ANABAPTIST-MENNONITE IDENTITIES IN FERMENT

LEO DRIEDGER AND LELAND HARDER

EDITORS

OCCASIONAL PAPERS NO. 14

Institute of Mennonite Studies
3003 Benham Avenue
Elkhart, Indiana 46517

1990

Occasional Papers

Occasional Papers is a publication of the Institute of Mennonite Studies and authorized by the Council of Mennonite Seminaries. The four sponsoring seminaries are Eastern Mennonite Seminary (Harrisonburg, VA), Goshen Biblical Seminary and Mennonite Biblical Seminary (Elkhart, IN), and the Mennonite Brethren Biblical Seminary (Fresno, CA). The Institute of Mennonite Studies is the research agency of the Associated Mennonite Biblical Seminaries.

Occasional Papers is released several times yearly without any prescribed calendar schedule. The purpose of the *Papers* is to make various types of essays available to foster dialogue in biblical, theological and practical ministry areas and to invite critical counsel from within the Mennonite theological community. While most essays will be in finished form, some may also be in a more germinal stage--released especially for purposes of testing and receiving critical feedback. In accepting papers for publication, priority will be given to authors from the CMS institutions, the college Bible faculties in the Council of Mennonite Colleges, the associate membership of the Institute of Mennonite Studies, and students and degree alumni of the four seminaries.

Because of limited circulation of the *Occasional Papers*, authors are free to use their material in other scholarly settings, either for oral presentation at scholarly meetings or for publication in journals with broader circulation and more official publication policies.

Orders for *Occasional Papers* should be sent to the Institute of Mennonite Studies, 3003 Benham Avenue, Elkhart, IN 46517-1999.

ISBN 0-936273-17-8
Printed in the U.S.A.

OTHER OCCASIONAL PAPERS BY THE INSTITUTE OF MENNONITE STUDIES:

No. 1 *Biblical Essays on War, Peace and Justice*   out of print

No. 2 *Theological Education in Missional Perspective*   out of print

No. 3 *The Bible and Law* $5.00

No. 4 *Following Jesus Christ in the World Today* $5.00
    (J. Moltmann)

No. 5 *The Pastor-People Partnership: The Call and Recall of Pastors from a Believer's Church Perspective* $5.00

No. 6 *Perspectives on the Nurturing of Faith* $5.00

No. 7 *Explorations of Systematic Theology* $5.00

No. 8 *Dialog Sequel to Moltmann's Following Jesus Christ in the World Today* $5.00

No. 9 *Essays on War and Peace: Bible and Early Church* $6.50

No. 10 *Perspectives on War and Peace: Bible and Early Church* $6.50

No. 11 *Essays on Spiritual Bondage and Deliverance* $8.00

No. 12 *Essays on Peace Theology and Witness* $8.00

No. 13 *A Disciple's Christology: Appraisals of Kraus's* Jesus Christ Our Lord $7.00

All prices listed are U.S. prices. Postage: add $1 for the first $10; .50 for each additional $10. To order any of these publications or to receive a complete listing of other IMS publications, please contact the Institute of Mennonite Studies, 3003 Benham Avenue, Elkhart, IN 46517-1999; 219/295-3726.

PREFACE

November 11-12, 1988 forty Mennonite and Brethren in Christ scholars gathered at the seminary in Elkhart, Indiana, for a consultation on the Church Member Profile II research project launched a year earlier by directors J. Howard Kauffman and Leland Harder and an Administrative Committee representing the five conferences involved in the study. Richard Kauffman and J. Howard Kauffman were the major organizers of the conference.

Two theologians and five sociologists presented major papers, with responses from sociologists, theologians, and historians, and extensive discussion of the presentations. The purpose of the consultation was to find new creative ways of conceptualizing a second North American social survey of Mennonites and Brethren in Christ called Church Member Profile II. A similar first survey was made in 1972 involving five conferences including the Brethren in Christ, the Mennonite Church, the General Conference Mennonite, Mennonite Brethren Church and the Evangelical Mennonite Church. *Anabaptists Four Centuries Later* was published by J. Howard Kauffman and Leland Harder in 1975, which has since become a major empirical reference.

The consultation was a stimulating meeting of older and younger scholars who debated the theories and methods of doing a second survey which would be both comparable to the first but also take into account new trends since 1972. The exchange between theologians and social scientists was so valuable that we thought it important to make these papers available to other interested readers. We thank Richard Kauffman and the Institute of Mennonite Studies for making the major presentations and responses available in print. We also thank Wilma Cender who helped organize the conference and who typed this volume.

The second North American survey was completed in 1989 and the data are presently being analyzed in preparation for the publication of two books. J. Howard Kauffman and Leo Driedger will write a scholarly volume similar to *Anabaptists Four Centuries Later* comparing the 1972 and 1989 trends. Leland Harder is preparing a volume to be used in church education classes for lay members of the church. In the meantime we present you with *Anabaptist-Mennonite Identities in Ferment*, which we trust will stimulate you as it did us.

Leo Driedger and Leland Harder, 1989

TABLE OF CONTENTS

DISCUSSING DIALECTICAL RENEWAL

      Peter M. Hamm 117

         Response by Lawrence M. Yoder 131
         Reply by Peter M. Hamm 133

6. Communal Commitment and Individualism
      Stephen C. Ainlay 135

         Response by Robert Enns 154

7. Identity and Assimilation
      Leo Driedger 159

         Response by Rodney Sawatsky 182
         Response by Jose Ortiz 187

INTRODUCTION

POLYMENNOS: IDENTITIES IN TRANSITION

Leo Driedger and Leland Harder

Advance printouts of the 1989 Church Member Profile II survey of Mennonites and Brethren in Christ in North America show that 48 percent are urban, living in centers of 2,500 or more; only seven percent are farmers. There are now four times as many Mennonites in the professions (27 percent) as working the land, a profound change since 1972 (Kauffman and Harder, 1975). As Mennonites urbanize, these changes are confounded by the influences of modernization, secularization, and assimilation in worlds where individualism and mainline Christianity are headed away from tradition, the sacred, the community, and identity. Can identities still be found in such a rush toward the melting pot? Do Mennonites still wish to be a leaven?

These were the questions asked by forty Mennonite and Brethren in Christ scholars when they met in November of 1988. Two theologians presented papers seeking to explore the early Anabaptist foundations and the pluralist trends in theological thinking today. Five sociologists focused on research of sectarianism in the past and the trends in modernization, secularization, individualism, and assimilation. The interchange between theologians and social scientists resulted in a dynamic encounter probing the dialectics of the sacred and the secular, the community and individualism, identity and assimilation. In this volume we share with you these papers and some of the responses. In this introduction we shall attempt to bring at least some sense of wholeness to what happens when Anabaptists turn into Mennonites fast becoming modern PolyMennos.

SORTING THEOLOGICAL PLURALISM

With increased urbanization and professionalism in North

America, the descendants of Anabaptists have become PolyMennos who see the world and their task differently than Mennonites prior to the seventies. Thus, our interpretation of the original Anabaptist movement has changed and our acceptance of many versions of being modern Anabaptists has also changed. The papers by Walter Klaassen and Norman Kraus illustrate these changes.

From Mono To Polygenesis

According to Walter Klaassen, 1975 was the watershed between two very important and distinct historical theological interpretations of the Anabaptist vision or visions. Harold Bender in the forties gathered Mennonite thinking into an Anabaptist vision which most scholars prior to the seventies embraced with deep appreciation. It was a monogenesis theory which according to Bender began with the Swiss Brethren in 1525 and spread elsewhere from this major center of Anabaptist activity. Bender, living in the small town of Goshen, Indiana, when most Mennonites were farmers in rural areas, sketched the monogenesis Anabaptist vision from a well integrated solid community basis, which appealed to like-positioned Mennonites of his day. *The* Anabaptist vision served all very well, especially since we had scattered to find our theologies before that at many wells, most of them not Anabaptist.

As Mennonites increasingly urbanized, moving away from small "Stillen-im-Lande" communities, we began to see that our urban ancestors, many who were mobile craftsmen, were more PolyAnabaptist than the Bender vision suggested. Walter Klaassen leads us into this polygenesis Anabaptist world.

Plural Theological Reconstruction Today

The change in our thinking from monogenesis to polygenesis has far-reaching implications for our theology. The urban pluralist environment constantly pushes us to rethink and reconstruct our theology previously dominated by the less changing rural environment and now influenced by the fast-moving urban settings where according to Reginald Bibby (1987) our Gods easily become fragmented, where servicing religious consumers *a la carte* is the trend. Participants in such secular, industrial, modern environments where individualism is king often have little interest in commitment, community, and service.

Norman Kraus outlines how our pluralist society has affected our need to reconstruct our theology for modern times. Numerous theological expressions have emerged which are centered around general orthodoxy, fundamentalism, evangelicalism, liberalism, and Anabaptism with their variations and modifications. Liberation theology, feminist theology, Black theology, as well as the charismatic movements must all be explored. Roman Catholic Christians are doing the same, and Mennonites often find kinship there, which in the sixteenth-century was inconceivable. Inter-Mennonite dialogue is taking place in many circles, and the range of differences within each conference is also noteworthy. New Mennonites have become PolyMennos so that Hispanics, Asians, Blacks and others are making their impact. Theological pluralism among Mennonites is increasing and the need for reconstruction is real. Kraus (1987) has recently published new views on Christology which have their defenders and detractors.

FINDING SOCIOLOGICAL ESSENTIALS

Two of the five sociologists who write in part two logically follow the two theological essays in part one. Calvin Redekop writes about some of the earliest sociological research done on Mennonites which focused on structural-functional sectarianism, and Donald Kraybill follows with his exploration of modernization, a major general factor in social change.

From Sectarian Boundaries to Open Denominationalism

Early sociologists like Max Weber and Ernst Troeltsch were interested in the changes which had been brought about by industrialization in Europe and its affect on religion. Early Mennonite sociologists like J. Winfield Fretz and Calvin Redekop used versions of the sect cycle in their research on the Old Colony and other Mennonites in Mexico, Paraguay, and North America. Like Bender in theology, these sociologists applied the structural-functional approach to describing rural Mennonite communities where social change was limited. They researched accommodation to mass society, mutual aid, the congregation, family and community.

Now that half of the Mennonites and Brethren in Christ have become urban, they are exposed to the larger society, no longer isolated in territorial and ethnic farm enclaves. Troeltsch predicted that sects modify their boundaries and slowly become more open to the society around them, and in the form of a sect-church cycle become more church-like. Leland Harder studied the General Conference Mennonites and decided that they had become an "established sect" moving toward denominationalism and future church-likeness. Redekop summarizes the debate over the years as to whether this sect-church typology is helpful in the study of Mennonites or not, and assesses what value this approach may have in the future.

Modernization and Differentiation

Classical theorists such as Marx, Weber, Toennies, Simmel, and Durkheim were all preoccupied with tracing the changes from a rural peasant to an industrial, urban society. These processes were described as moving from *gemeinschaft* to *gesellschaft*, from mechanical to organic solidarity and from a homogeneous to a more differentiated life. Now that Mennonites have fully entered all facets of modern society they too are faced with similar changes.

Donald Kraybill reviews the various characteristics used to describe modernization such as differentiation of occupations and work, the collection of diverse groups in cities often referred to as cultural pluralism, rationalization and bureaucratization involving more rules and hierarchies of status, increasing secondary ties, emphases on the individual in contrast to more secure primary communities, secularization, abstraction, rapid change, more need for choice, tolerance, and increasing uncertainty. It is clear that while modernization with its technology often offers a higher standard of income, the social costs in loss of security, identification with work, and general life satisfaction are sometimes considerable.

Hunter (1983:130) concluded that evangelicalism thrives best the *farther away* it is located from the key structural pressures of modernity-urbanization, high levels of education, high mobility-producing income levels, and the bureaucratic spheres of work. Is this true also of Anabaptism? Was there no truth at all in Paul Peachey's (1955:82) hypothesis that "if the genius of Anabaptism is the creation and perpetuation of the distinctly religious community, and is thus involved in social heterogeneity, then the urban environment (i.e., precisely where the forces of modernity are strongest) provides a more congenial setting for a vital Anabaptism than does the rural?"

The research is clear that the trend is away from sectarianism and tradition in the direction of denominationalism and modernization as Mennonites become more urban and professional. Part three explores what becomes of Mennonites as "A People," as they increasingly leave their traditional moorings and compete in the larger society.

DISCUSSING DIALECTICAL RENEWAL

Part one suggests that the early Anabaptists clearly separated themselves from the state church to form new fellowships and that today theological pluralism is on the rise in search of religious meaning in a fast changing society. Part two reviews major trends away from sectarianism toward denominationalism and differentiation as modernization has greatly influenced Mennonites. Part three introduces three papers which deal with the dialectic between the sacred and the secular, commitment and individualism, and identity and assimilation. This dialectic seems to be a back and forth oscillating between two poles constantly interacting with each other, forming modified and changed forms of the sacred, commitment, and identity.

The Sacred and Secularization

Peter Hamm goes back to the basics of defining religion in a broader context, reflecting the way his travels as a foreign mission secretary for the Mennonite Brethren Church have taken him into many Muslim, Buddhist, Confusianist, and Taoist settings. What are the issues which relate to the creation of "meaning" in the many world settings as well as the new urban setting in which Mennonites now find themselves? He discusses "the sacred" as a process of sacralization in opposition to secularization which is also a process away from the sacred. Sacralization and secularization are processes, not static concepts, which interact with each other in a complex dialectic. Sometimes it is difficult to determine which is the dominant force.

The English word *secular* derives from the Latin *saeculum*, meaning "this present age." Thus the vocation of a secular priest as one who lived and served in the world was distinguished from the "religious priest," who lived apart in a cloister "contemplating the changeless order of holy truth" (Cox, 1965:15). In this sense, the sixteenth century Anabaptists were radical secularists who proposed that the laity, the church out in the world, should become the carriers of the faith, the connecting link between the gospel and the world. If the world is where we belong, how do we distinguish between being "in the world" and yet "not of the world" (John 17:11,14)? In his book on the myth of secularism, Edwin Aubrey (1954:30-31) writes that "the whole history of the Christian movement exhibits an alternation between periods of *diastole*, when Christianity reaches out into culture to absorb elements which it may use for the enrichment of its own life and thought, and *systole*, when the church draws into itself in a contractive movement which tries to exclude cultural forces so as to recover its own uniqueness."

The dialectic between opposite forces creates a different view and approach to religion. The "in but not of the world" stance becomes real because now the world is no longer defined in separate boundaried boxes as Mennonites were prone to do in rural ethnic enclaves, but faith and life must be negotiated and lived in a changing crucible of interaction. Constant selection and alert opening and closing to new experiences are needed. A sense of direction, clarity of vision, being committed to some features of society and not to others, becomes part of the quest for meaning. Old forms may decline in favor of newer more relevant ones which emerge. Thus, "the sacred" is found within the processes of secularization, rather than in secluded separation. The sacred and secular are in touch with each other, sufficiently different so that they are in constant dialectical conflict with each other because they are headed in opposite directions.

In Search of "Genuine" Individualism

Is individualism what Bellah and associates (1985) call *ontological*: the view that with an inalienable inherent dignity the individual has a prior existence to that of the group? By this definition, the group comes into existence only through the voluntary contract of individuals trying to maximize their own self interest. Or is the biblical view, which makes the individual and the covenant community cognate creations of God, the normative vision for our study? And how do we see biblical individualism vis-a-vis ontological/utilitarian individualism? When is the church's expectations of its members biblical--a kind of self interest in reverse? Stephen Ainlay builds his whole discussion around Bellah's *Habits of the Heart* (1985) and insists that there must be a balance, a tension between the individual and community of which the person is a part. "While they do not celebrate individualism (as Adam Smith did), neither do they seem to agonize over it (as did Weber)," Ainlay says about Bellah and associates. Inasmuch as individualism lies at the core of North American culture, we can hardly abandon it because it is part of our deepest identity.

Ainlay discusses four types of individualism (biblical, civic, utilitarian and expressive), and he suggests that the first two are "genuine" and the last two pathological. In the case of biblical and civic individualism there are higher causes to relate to so it does not contribute to fragmentism but helps build the larger social whole. It is important that individualism is held in check in this manner, because the two pathological forms of utilitarian and expressive individualism are centered too much on the self with its negative potential for pride, greed, and self gratification as ends in themselves.

Holding individualism in check so it can be used toward larger religious and civic goals is essential, which leads us to a discussion of identity and its many complex forms of expression.

Finding Identity in the Melting Pot

The central focus of the Anabaptist quest was renewal of a commitment to God and restoration of a new community of believers as found in the records of the early church. Peter Hamm explores what such identification with the sacred means today. Stephen Ainlay shows that the modern trend is toward individualism rather than commitment to a religious community, and tries to sort out the difference between "genuine" individualism which serves others and pathological individualism which serves the self. Both Hamm and Ainlay suggest that there is a dialectical relationship between the sacred and the secular, the individual and the community. This is also the case in developing self identity and group identity; both complement each other but are also in tension with each other as well as in conflict with the larger modern society.

Theorists of assimilation assume that the marketplace and modern industrial opportunities will seduce religious and cultural groups sucking them into the mainstream where they will lose their original identity and want to become like others. As Mennonites move from rural cultural enclaves to the city, theorists like Gordon suggest that they will give up their language and culture, marry non-Mennonites, begin to identify with others in their attitudes and behavior and assimilate into the larger mainstream melting pot, no longer distinguishable from the sect.

Other pluralist theorists claim that some like Jews, Hutterites, Doukhobors, Mormons, French Canadians, Native Indians, and Inuit will not assimilate. Religion, race, and language, some say, can become important foci to which groups commit themselves, so they will not assimilate but perpetuate a distinctive identity. Driedger discusses territory, minority institutions, ethnic culture, historic symbols, ideology and leadership as important factors around which minorities have built their identity.

The early Anabaptists focused their new identity mostly around a renewed Christian ideology and leadership which launched their Anabaptist identity. Later, religious fervor declined, replaced by territorially separated communities where they maintained their own schools, churches and work. Swiss, Dutch, and German language and culture loomed large in their identification. The Amish and Hutterites are good modern examples. Recently, some emergent urban Mennonite groups have again concentrated more on their distinct religious ideology, historic Anabaptist symbols (the Anabaptist Vision), and leadership educated in Mennonite schools. Identity has shifted over the years, although religion has always been an important focus.

FINDING AN INTEGRATIVE MODEL FOR CHANGE

Given our Anabaptist pluralist polygenesis beginnings and our pluralistic theological tendencies today, how can we summarize what is happening to us? Sectarianism, which worked in rural areas, is on the decline and modernization is running its course among Mennonites today. Can we suggest how these dialectical processes between the sacred and secular, individualism and community responsibility, and identity and assimilation work together toward an Anabaptist and Mennonite future? In Figure 1 we present a summary model which hopefully will help the reader to find the way in the maze of change which is presented in the seven papers and the responses which follow. Each line in the figure originates in the basic concepts of one of the papers.

So far we are suggesting that what it means to be a Mennonite involves at least seven dimensions which the papers address, and that together they form a modality (common high points) which we call Mennonite. What we mean by Mennonite identity, then, is a common modality which has developed over 460 years, which has changed over time, and which manifests a range of options within that modality. Thus we may find a variety of Mennonite expressions within that modality, but the general model is moving in a direction of identification with the sacred, a community, a tradition which we still call Anabaptist, some aspects of which are sect-like and others church-like.

In Figure 1 we show the radicalization process away from the civic (state) church toward renewed Anabaptism which took place in the sixteenth century. That pluralization is also at work today (shown in the second continuum), generated by new forms of liberal, fundamentalist, neorthodox, evangelical, feminist, and liberation theologies, all of which influence us (differently for each individual) in our theological pluralism today.

Whereas the first two continua direct us away from the large society, the next two clearly move from sectarianism toward society and denominationalism and from tradition toward modernity. All four processes influence all Mennonites and BICs, but not in the same way nor in the same proportions depending on social conditions.

The last three continua clearly show the dialectical processes at

Figure 1. Theological, Sociological and Dialectical Trends
Among Mennonites

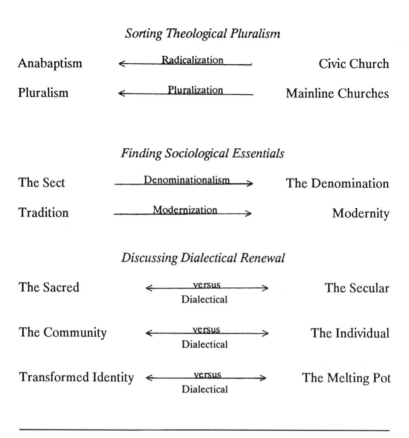

Sorting Theological Pluralism

| Anabaptism | ←————Radicalization———— | Civic Church |
| Pluralism | ←————Pluralization———— | Mainline Churches |

Finding Sociological Essentials

| The Sect | ————Denominationalism———→ | The Denomination |
| Tradition | ————Modernization———→ | Modernity |

Discussing Dialectical Renewal

The Sacred	←————versus————→ Dialectical	The Secular
The Community	←————versus————→ Dialectical	The Individual
Transformed Identity	←————versus————→ Dialectical	The Melting Pot

work where these major poles (represented in the first four continua), slug-it-out in the marketplace and social arena. The sacred is
in conflict with the secular, the individual wants to be freed from
community pressures, and we all are in search of transformed
identities seeking to be saved from the melting pot of anonymity,
anomie, and lovelessness. Urban Mennonites especially, where
change is greatest, are in search of roots, in search of meaning in the
quest for individual fulfillment, seeking to find a sense of place, of
being, of belonging, of commitment, and of inspiration. The papers
that follow belong to the quest for such new life.

REFERENCES

Aubrey, Edwin E.
1954 *Secularity A Myth: An Examination of the Current Attack on Secularism.* New York: Harper and Brothers.

Bellah, R. N., *et al.*
1985 *Habits of the Heart.* Berkeley: University of California Press.

Cox, Harvey.
1965 *The Secular City.* New York: Macmillan.

Hunter, James Davison
1983 *American Evangelicalism.* New Brunswick, N. J.: Rutgers University Press.

Kauffman, J. Howard and Leland Harder
1975 *Anabaptists Four Centuries Later.* Scottdale, PA: Herald Press.

Kraus, C. Norman
1987 *Jesus Christ Our Lord: Christology from a Disciple's Perspective.* Scottdale, PA: Herald Press.

Peachey, Paul
1955 "Early Anabaptists and Urbanism." In *Proceedings of the Tenth Conference on Mennonite Educational and Cultural Problems.* Chicago: Mennonite Biblical Seminary.

SORTING THEOLOGICAL PLURALISM

CHAPTER 1

THE QUEST FOR ANABAPTIST IDENTITY

Walter Klaassen

The wording of the title is based on the conviction that the Mennonite tradition is important and that it is something that should be preserved. But what parts should be preserved and how? This preservation process has two facets. The first has to do with memory--to know our history, to know what happened in the sixteenth century, to know the people who were represented at its beginning, and to know what they stood for and what their views were about the things that came to characterize the Mennonite tradition. The second has to do with continuity, how the tradition expresses itself today. Anabaptism cannot simply be transplanted from the sixteenth to the twentieth century. One obvious difference is that we in North America are not persecuted today and can therefore hardly be called Anabaptists in that sense. Being Anabaptist in that other century was virtually synonymous with being persecuted. What parts of the tradition should be preserved today if we are to involve ourselves in the ongoing Anabaptist movement? What features of that movement, preserved today, will mark us in the eyes of other Christians as belonging to that tradition?

To answer our queries, a brief history of the writing of the Anabaptist story is needed. In 1975 an essay was published in the *Mennonite Quarterly Review* with the curious title: "From Monogenesis to Polygenesis: The Historical Discussion of Anabaptist Origins" (Stayer, Packull and Depperman, 1975). None of the three authors was a Mennonite. James M. Stayer and Werner O. Packull were Canadians, and Klaus Depperman was German. That essay marked a turning-point in the understanding of sixteenth-century Anabaptism. It was a revision of the view normally associated with Harold S. Bender of Goshen College that Anabaptism, having started in Zürich, gradually spread from Switzerland through western Europe as a single uniform movement (Bender, 1944). This understanding of Anabaptism promoted the view that within the movement there was a common solid core of beliefs, with softer expressions of its main affirmations farther away from the center, and even degenerating into perversions at the circumference. The solid core was represented by the Swiss Brethren, the Hutterites, and the followers of Menno Simons, and was referred to by Bender as "evangelical Anabaptism." Up to 1975 that model was taken for granted by all who were taught by Harold Bender and George H. Williams (Williams, 1962).

But now that has all changed and a different model or paradigm has taken the place of Bender's vision. This revised model, first developed by Stayer, rejected the claim that Anabaptism had spread more or less intact from Zürich to the rest of Europe. Instead, it was observed that Anabaptism arose in three areas-- Switzerland, South Germany, and the Netherlands--mostly independent of each other exhibiting distinct characteristics in each place (Stayer 1972). To identify the three groupings we could say that the Swiss Brethren were Zwinglian-humanist, i.e., that they were at many points followers of the Reformation ideas of the Zürich Reformer Huldrych Zwingli and of the humanist ideas stemming from Erasmus of Rotterdam. The South German Anabaptists were mystical-humanist, i.e., they had been strongly influenced by the thinking of the great German mystics of the Middle Ages and also by the humanism of Erasmus. The Netherlands Anabaptists were sacramentarian-apocalyptic, i.e., they were shaped by a Dutch tradition which understood the bread and wine of the Lord's Supper to be symbolic of the body and blood of Jesus, rather than the actual body and blood, and were also characterized in a special way by the late medieval conviction that they were living in the end times and that they had a special role in those events (Klaassen, 1986). Thus, from the view of a single source for Anabaptism, *mongenesis*, we came to the view of several sources, *polygenesis*. This revision has, since 1975, quickly established itself as the more adequate and reliable model.

The Bender model of a single source and a single movement with three clearly identifiable characteristics--the essence of Christianity as discipleship, the church as a brotherhood, and a new ethic of love and nonresistance--made relatively simple the matter of what in the tradition we can use today. It was clear that those three central beliefs were as relevant to our century as they were to the sixteenth. But when you have at least three movements with a variety of emphases, it's not so simple. Still, it is not impossible, and that is because of another, equally important part of the new model.

All three Anabaptist groupings were part of a pervasive European protest movement of lay people against being controlled by the clergy (Goertz, 1980:41-76). Martin Luther's teaching of the priesthood of all believers, i.e., that every Christian could and should do what had until then been reserved only for the clergy, had done its work well. People believed it, and proceeded to read and explain the Bible to each other and to decide for themselves what the most important parts of Christian belief were. The priests, they said, could not be trusted in their teaching because they did not demonstrate Christian teaching in their lives. Anabaptism was the most visible churchly expression of that movement. As it developed in the various areas it expressed its anticlericalism in very similar ways. The fundamental demand of the popular movement was that control of church leadership should be in the hands of the local people in the parish. Anabaptists everywhere concluded that such leadership would have to be lay leadership. Given that conclusion, a certain similarity among the various groups resulted even though they sometimes differed widely on other issues.

The earliest years of the movement in Switzerland, 1524-1527, in South Germany, 1526-1528, and in the Netherlands, 1530-1536, were years of considerable turmoil and searching for direction. Consolidation came in Switzerland in 1527 with the Schleitheim Articles, in South Germany with the failure of Hans Hut's prediction of Christ's return at Pentecost, 1528, and in the Netherlands soon after the fall of Münster in June, 1535. After that there was a convergence among the groups as they developed, their popular anticlericalism in large measure determining the shape they gave to their church structures. Differences persisted, but Bender saw correctly a central core of convictions that united them, but he pushed that central core too far into the beginnings.

The writer has no intention of refuting the validity of what Harold Bender identified as the heart of the tradition. It was a legitimate way of characterizing Anabaptism, it continues to inform our thinking, and the reader will notice that it is not absent in my further analysis. But I am not H. S. Bender, and the year is 1990, not 1942. By this I mean to say that the times in which we write Anabaptist history help to determine what we see in that history. Harold Bender wanted to do at least two things in 1942, when as the president of the American Society of Church History, he delivered his presidential address which he called "The Anabaptist Vision." First he set out to convince other Christians that Anabaptism was part of the Reformation, in fact a part that had taken the Reformation to its proper conclusion. Secondly, he wanted to chart a path for American Mennonites between "modernism" and "fundamentalism." Anabaptism, as he saw correctly, was neither, and therefore admirably suited to help Mennonites in their self-identity at that time. It is my judgment that he was highly successful on both counts (Sawatsky, 1977).

Since 1942 we have entered the nuclear age and more recently have come face to face with the equally threatening world-wide ecological degradation. Since 1942 secularization has made serious inroads into Mennonite churches of all stripes in North America. Hence my description of what in Anabaptism is relevant today will look somewhat different from Harold Bender's. In any given time and circumstance we will choose those tenets which speak most adequately to our time.

It is important to reiterate that we must not regard either the Anabaptists or their time as modern, nor as belonging to our time. They emphatically belonged to another century when things were not as they are today. When people became Anabaptists in the sixteenth century they were not making a denominational choice; there were no denominations. They were also not making a religious choice; they remained Christians. They were not joining a convenient, congenial group; they did not have that luxury in a hard time. They did not become Anabaptists for family, social, traditional, ethnic, or political reasons. But all of these are reasons people cite today for joining a Mennonite church. Keep this warning in mind as I continue.

Sixteenth century Anabaptism is very important to the Mennonite churches today and I say that because of what I believe about history. As a Christian I believe that God reveals himself in human history. The history of the church is just as revealing as biblical history. How and what it reveals depends very much on the interpreters of that history. It's very much like scriptural interpretation. Over the centuries Christians have derived opposing views of human affairs from scripture. That Christians could be defenders of every kind of political system and every use of coercion and violence ever invented reflects not a neglect of scripture but a particular reading of it. That trinitarians and unitarians both appeal to the same Bible may not be attributed to ignorance or perverseness but to the nature of the scriptures themselves, as well as to the times and conditions under which the interpreters spoke. The same applies to our reading of human history since scriptural times. How, given the witches brew of good and evil that has been western history since the cross, can we trace the revelation of God in it?

We are considering the Mennonite community through time back to its specific beginnings in the sixteenth century, but not in isolation. Our history is part of the history of the church which began specifically with the resurrection but which really goes all the way back to Abraham's exodus from Ur of the Chaldees. We can say categorically that the incarnation of God in Christ and the teachings of the New Testament represent the foundation of the church. Every Christian group from Roman Catholic to the latest Protestant splinter has sought to anchor itself in the beginnings which are recorded in the New Testament writings. Subsequent developments in the life of the church are judged by that standard. When, therefore, we come to our own tradition, and assume it still to be important and relevant, we use the same rules even if its specific origins came long after the beginnings of Christianity itself. In that sense we are in the same boat with the Lutheran, Anglican, and Reformed traditions. Some, like Baptists, Methodists, Pentecostalists and others, are even more recent than ours. What we cling to in our tradition is basically a certain way of interpreting the biblical evidence relating to our faith, and we have maintained that relatively intact through the centuries to the present.

It is not difficult, therefore, to argue that the tenets of sixteenth century Anabaptism are central for the Mennonite churches of today, and to acknowledge that the *whole* tradition is ours from Zwickau to Zürich, from Münster to Melk, and from Amsterdam to Augsburg. And because the Anabaptist tradition was so varied and diverse, we will have to make choices even within our own tradition. For none of us can hold to both Armageddon and nonresistance, to both a rigid and a lenient church discipline, to both God and Satan as the source of governmental authority. And yet all of these were part of the Anabaptist tradition. Not everything in the tradition was good or according to our present understanding of scripture. As we choose, then, we will use the scriptures, the subsequent tradition of our church, and the traditions of other churches as the criteria by which we choose. If we continue to see ourselves as heir to the historical tradition of Anabaptists and Mennonites, then we will listen to that tradition as we evaluate trends in contemporary Mennonite life, thought, and action, and as we do so we will also listen very carefully to the experience of other traditions past and present. The principle of *ecclesia semper reformanda*--the church always reforming itself--applies to us too.

Which aspects of sixteenth century Anabaptism can therefore be considered vital for today, and which not? I insist that they all are. God reveals himself in history, by means of which we are taught. We should have the courage of the Old Testament writers who did not hesitate to blame their ancestors for unfaithfulness, even as they praised them for their faith. We listen, therefore, to both the positive and the negative, always remembering to make proper allowances for differences in social, religious, and political settings between then and now. We can learn from the whole spectrum of ideas and actions. Our understanding of the gospel will determine what parts of the tradition we receive as contributing to our faithfulness today and what parts we reject as contrary to the gospel. Three perspectives for the discerning process are ecumenical theology (that is a theology accepted by all Christians), a theology of grace and obedience, and the call to a mature Christian faith.

ECUMENICAL THEOLOGY

Earlier interpreters of Anabaptism saw clearly what we today often miss, i.e., that sixteenth century Anabaptists, on the whole, accepted the ancient Christian symbols which identified orthodox Christian belief. Even the somewhat strange Christology of Dutch Anabaptism could be held without repudiating the Apostles' Creed. This adherence to the basic theological affirmations of the ancient church represents a truly massive dependence upon church tradition by Anabaptists, a confession of continuity with the past, and even if often unwillingly, a confession that they shared this tradition with their contemporaries. The Apostles' Creed, especially, was often used by Anabaptists as a way of stating the basic faith when asked about their belief (Friedmann, 1967:21-36). There are numerous examples, e.g., (Riedemann, 1951:15-16) Leonhard Schiemer (Muller, 1938:44-58), Menno Simons (Wenger, 1956:487-498, 525, 703, 754, 761), and an anonymous Anabaptist confession (Hillerbrand, 1959:40-50). The evidence is overwhelming, and the basic Anabaptist theological orthodoxy (proper belief) should not be obscured by the highlighting of their orthopraxis (proper practice) which is the other part of their system. Their adherence to basic, orthodox church theology came not by default as is sometimes implied, but by deliberate documentation in that all the basic affirmations were massively biblically based.

That emphasis on traditional trinitarian theology with its expansion in the Apostles' Creed was not a matter of secondary importance. This transcendent reference was absolutely essential as the matrix out of which grew their dynamic Christology and the resulting view of discipleship as an integral part of the faith that justifies. Without trinitarian faith there would have been no Anabaptism. People like Menno Simons were sophisticated enough to know that the Apostles' Creed was not a New Testament document, and certainly not the Nicene Creed.

Trinitarian theology remains a very important tenet of Anabaptism that is relevant for today. We desperately need links to the tradition of the church which transcends the Mennonite churches, and as a recognition that our tradition was not a brand new departure but very much a part of the rest of Christianity, however much that Christianity was criticized and rejected by sixteenth-century Anabaptists.

The transcendent anchorage of a trinitarian theology is absolutely essential today, for if we don't have it, we will get lost in the relativities of history and culture. Unless we are guided ultimately by that confession with its symbolization in worship and the Lord's Supper, we will not be able to resist the secularism that even now is deeply entrenched in our souls.

A THEOLOGY OF GRACE AND OBEDIENCE

This subject is best treated in two parts. The first is that divine grace is expressed in *conversion and baptism*. A theology of grace meant that God was prior to all. The process of conversion did not begin in man. God sent the Word, Jesus, into the world as judgment on human sin and pride. The acceptance of that judgment was a conversion which included remorse for sin, repentance, and a joyful embracing of the liberation God offered. It was the grace of God alone that made possible the human response, and that response was a yes to God's generosity. The joy of release energized and directed the convert toward the new life of obedience to God's will. Believing in God through Christ was therefore defined only by repentance, faith, and the new life of obedience to Christ. All other criteria of birth, family, territory, education, etc., were rejected. That gracious divine initiative and that joyful human response were symbolized in baptism. I will come back to that subject at another point.

Conversion, repentance, and forgiveness identify a consciousness of having entered into a relationship with God the Creator and Redeemer, the one who holds each of his own in his caring hands and who holds in those same hands the issues of human history on this planet. It means being linked to all that is, a consciousness of being part of God's dependent creation, but called by God as caretaker of it. It is a great and sublime destiny. Can we, in the everydayness of church life, instill and nurture that consciousness, the wonder of our high calling in Jesus Christ? It is basic to all the rest of our life. If it is not there, we will share in and contribute to the general despair, and we will not be light, salt, or yeast (Matt. 5:13-16; 13:33).

The second is that obedience is the outworking of *the sanctification of life*. Anabaptists were convinced that the acceptance by God of the repentant sinner was not an imparting of righteousness as Luther taught. He was convinced that righteous actions or good works were evidence of true faith, but that they had no weight or intrinsic importance in God's economy. For Anabaptists the union of believing and accepting God's offer and promises and the resultant works of faith, together, constituted saving faith. It was a central tenet of the tradition and essential to it. But it was a difficult one to handle, because once doing became a part of believing, the tendency was to concentrate on that at the expense of trusting solely in God's grace. That is what Luther criticized in late medieval theology and rejected without qualification also in Anabaptism because it destroyed human dependence on God.

Still, this emphasis on doing the works of faith most caught people's attention in the sixteenth century. The new living according to the scriptures, the actual doing of God's will in one's daily life, made the Anabaptist communities very attractive to people. The Reformers complained that often the people who left their churches to go over to Anabaptism were the people most concerned about godly living. Political and churchly authorities often found themselves frustrated in prosecuting Anabaptists because local officials said that it was wrong to imprison and kill such good Christians. Following the footsteps of Jesus, the Son of God, was as important as the Anabaptists' confession with the mouth that Jesus is the Son of God.

But having said that, it is also important to say that our belief in the sanctified life is the one we've suffered under the most. We have striven for personal and communal holiness and in that competition have caused disunity, schism, personal guilt, and an often censorious spirit. We partake of the problems of every community that strives for perfection, the liberals among us quite as much as the conservatives. The striving for the perfect program for world peace has driven the peace movement into competing sects. It's no different in the ecological movement. We've seen the same thing in Marxism in the attempt to out-Lenin Lenin by Mao Tse Tung of China, Pol Pot of Kampuchea, and the Albanians. Such competitive striving for perfection whether among Christians or Marxists is not evidence of holiness but of human pride, and that is part of our sixteenth century heritage that we should leave behind for good. Whenever works of faith turn into works of merit, the gospel is being denied.

THE CALL TO A MATURE CHRISTIAN FAITH

This is a discussion of the Anabaptist view of the church, their attitude to society, the use of the scriptures, and their Christian witness.

The Church of Believers

For Anabaptists the Christian believer was not isolated. Baptism was baptism into the church and not a private transaction between the believer and God. It was the commitment to the disciplined community which strengthened, encouraged, and helped the believer to live the life of discipleship. But again, the church was much more than an adjunct to the personal struggle. In the church the believer was in a special way in touch with the source of faith through the Lord's Supper, worship, Bible study and admonition. In it was shaped the believer's new view of the church and reality.

The church itself is to be not simply a cadre of party workers, but a sign of hope to the world, since it is God's colony in the world. It is the laboratory of the new liberated life in the world. It is a workshop of Kingdom living, a school for the development of the habits and mindset of the spirit of love and forgiveness and patience with the world's sin and blindness. The longer one describes the vision of what the church is to be, the more discouraged one is apt to become since it so rarely reaches the ideal. That is exactly why the church is an article of faith in the Creed: "I believe in the holy, universal church, the communion of saints." I believe in its possibility, that it can in fact be light, salt and yeast, that it can be the community in which people can find security, in which they are constantly directed to God as the author of all we have and are; but we never achieve that ideal. Still, the church is more important than ever in our time when God has been banned from the world, when secular, often destructive, symbols dominate the life of homes, communities and nations. It is more important than ever that those symbols are not allowed to invade the church, the community of the disciples of Christ, in which the cross, water, bread and wine remain the perennial and irreplaceable Word of God to us and the world.

Anticlericalism, Baptism, and the Critique of Church and Society

Anabaptism was in its time, as already noted, part of a much larger, quite amorphous movement of popular anticlericalism. Its aim was to throw off the shackles of clerical control because they had lost confidence in the clergy as dependable spiritual guides, first the Catholic clergy, and very soon those of the "new evangelicals" (by which they meant those who were later called Protestants) as well. Mostly lay people, Anabaptists were prepared to take into their hands what had for over a millennium been reserved strictly for the clergy.

But how could lay people qualify? How could they do it? This question led in Zürich to the view that for a church of lay people to function they would have to begin to baptize only adult believers. Thus, members of the church were only those who were believers by choice and were ready to witness to their faith in a hostile world. Certainly the biblical evidence also drove them in that direction. Thus baptism became the seal of personal faith, of submission to the discipline of the community of faith and the commissioning to witness in the world. The discerning and understanding of what was happening around them in their time called for spiritual maturity. Thus Anabaptists disputed that Europe was Christian just because everyone was baptized. They challenged the notion of the time that the church was territorial and bounded by political jurisdictions, or that the church was defined by political agreements. They questioned the existing economic arrangements in Europe which they said were exploitive. They challenged and repudiated the view that Christians could in good conscience participate in the prevailing official violence and coercion of the day. For all that, mature believers were needed, believers who were conscious that they had received grace from God and had been empowered by his Spirit.

Sola Scriptura with a Difference

In the scriptures Anabaptists found the good news of God's forgiveness but also extensive prescriptions for the nature of the new life. The basic principle of scriptural interpretation was the "life and doctrine of Christ and the Apostles" (Klaassen, 1984). The lowliness of Christ with its humility and its renunciation of coercive power became the model for the believer (Klassen and Klaassen, 1978:428-63), and that required immersion in the model by acquaintance with the Bible. The scriptures also supplied the trenchant critique of injustice and oppression, especially found in the prophets of the Old Testament. Their use of the scriptures led to radical nonconformity. Study of the scriptures in the congregation of believers provided a common understanding of both church and world.

Today in our culture we have our own clerics. They are the people who run our society, the technical experts, the managers, the technocrats. These are our priests, and they do all they can to keep us under their control. Their view of the world and their freedom to do as they please depends on our ignorance. Lay people, we are told, can't understand the complicated issues of nuclear power, of national defense, of human and planetary ecology, of biotechnology, of the mysteries of medical science, etc. *But they can,* and it is in the community of faith that they become literate in these matters. There they learn to identify and expose the numerous modern superstitions which underlie and energize our culture, such as for example, the idea that peace can be created and maintained by weapons, or that our planet can sustain unlimited economic growth. The baptized believers are the ones who throw off the tutelage and control of these new priests, because not these priests, but Jesus is Lord; not they, but the Lord is the arbiter of history. Baptism could, therefore, again become an act of nonconformity, a sign of the rejection of the clerics of our time who are as unreliable and exploitive as were the clergy our ancestors rejected 450 years ago.

The chief source for the believers' understanding are the scriptures, not, to be sure, for the specifics of science and technology, but for exposing the underlying superstitions of our time for the frauds they are, and for learning what goes in their place once they have been exposed. That requires a massive job of what we normally call adult education, not as an adjunct to the Sunday School for children so the parents have something to do while the kids are in class, but as a structured, planned program that goes beyond the one lesson quarterly that is normally provided for adults. Don't adults also advance, so that there should be a series of perhaps a dozen such courses, each building on the other in an activity, unremitting and sophisticated, that equips believers for engagement with the world? And that could have an interesting by-product, namely, that such educated parents could then teach their children--a novel idea that is today virtually nonexistent.

Every Member a Witness

Because Anabaptism was a lay and not a clerical movement, every believer was, in essence, a priest, a minister. That view was central to the Reformation in Wittenberg, Zürich, Geneva, and Canterbury from the beginning, but it was taken further by Anabaptists than by anyone else. And since every believer was a minister, every believer had to be equipped to witness. A believer could not be a witness without a profound sense of being a believer by personal choice, by baptism, by Bible study, by congregational process. It was the secret of Anabaptism's growth.

The identification and training of every member as a witness is very important today because of its great flexibility and effectiveness. Our institutional forms of church planting and church growth are clumsy and cumbersome, and, by comparison, ineffective. The presence in any neighborhood of people who are well informed about current issues and who know how to talk about them from the perspective of the gospel; of people who are calm in the midst of apprehension and fear and confident in the midst of confusion; of people who know what they believe in a time of profound uncertainty and who undergird all that with a quiet and confident and loving spirit; such people will do more for God's cause in the world than all the technologically correct methods of institution-building.

SUMMARY

All of this constitutes a call to nonconformity with the world. I've tried to identify some specific paths of nonconformity. Let me underscore them again.

Baptism, we need to remind ourselves, was at the beginning throughout the movement an act of civil disobedience. It was against the law. It was a political act of high visibility. We should really allow that fact to sink in. One who was baptized back in 1530 was liable to be arrested and charged with breaking the law. Being baptized was an act which said that here was a person who put in question many of the basic assumptions of the time which were regarded as unchallengeable and as part of the Christian view of things. Being baptized was not simply a symbolic way of saying "I love Jesus and Jesus loves me." By being baptized one became a part of God's bridgehead in the world, and that meant taking on the world and its error, not running away from it. The demands of this new life direction were so high that they could never be carried out unless people knew they were part of the movement of history which was being directed by God.

This new life began as trust in God through repentance and forgiveness and was sealed by baptism. It was submission to the transforming work of the Holy Spirit which produced a change of attitude and action that rejected all coercive domination and violence. Basic was an ecumenical theology of creation and redemption by incarnation.

The congregation was the visible expression of the new human community redeemed from fear and greed. It expressed its own dependence on God through worship and the Lord's Supper. In it believers were nurtured to maturity where they learned how to speak to the pressing issues of the day. In it they studied the scriptures together intensively and so received the vision and the support for challenging the clerics of their day without fear.

That ordinary lay people should do this was taken for granted, for by definition every believer was a witness to the gospel.

REFERENCES

Bender Harold S.
1944 "The Anabaptist Vision." *Church History* 18:3-24.

Friedmann, Robert (Ed.)
1967 *Glaubenszeugnisse Oberdeutscher Taufgesinnter* II. Gutersloher Verlagshaus Gerd Mohn.

Goertz, Hans-Jurgen
1980 *Die Täufer: Geschichte und Deutung.* München: Beck.

Hillerbrand, Hans J.
1959 "Ein Tauferbekenntnis aus dem 16. Jahrhundert." *ARG* 50:40-50.

Klaassen, Walter
1984 "Anabaptist Hermeneutics: Presuppositions, Principles and Practice." In Willard Swartley (Ed.), *Essays on Biblical Interpretation*. Elkhart: Institute of Mennonite Studies, 5-10.

Klaassen, Walter
1986 "Eschatological Themes in Early Dutch Anabaptism." In Irvin B. Horst (Ed.), *Dutch Dissenters*. Brill: 15-31.

Klassen, William and Walter Klaassen
1978 *The Writings of Pilgram Marpeck.* Scottdale: Herald Press.

Muller, H.
1938 *Glaubenszeugnisse Oberdeutscher Taufgesinnter.* Leipzig.

Rideman, Peter
1951 *Peter Rideman: Account of our Religion, Doctrine and Faith*, translated by K. Hasenberg. London: Hodder and Stoughton.

Sawatsky, Rodney J.
1977 "History and Ideology: American Mennonite Identity Definition through History." Princeton, N.J.: Unpublished Ph.D. Dissertation, Princeton University.

Stayer, James M.
　　1972 *Anabaptists and the Sword*. Lawarence, Kansas:
　　　　　Coronado Press.

Stayer, James M., Werner Packull and Klaus Depperman
　　1975 "From Monogenesis to Polygenesis: The Historical Dis-
　　　　　cussion of Anabaptist Origins." *Mennonite Quarterly
　　　　　Review* 49:83-121.

Wenger, John C.
　　1956 *The Complete Writings of Menno Simons*. Scottdale:
　　　　　Herald Press.

Williams, George H.
　　1962 *The Radical Reformation*. Philadelphia: Westminster
　　　　　Press.

RESPONSE

J. Denny Weaver

The task of Walter Klaassen was to tell us what aspects of
sixteenth-century Anabaptism, the historical movement to which
modern Mennonite groups can trace their roots, are relevant for
Mennonites in the twentieth century.
That is an appropriate task. As we all recognize, it is in a
movement's origins that we discover a movement's raison d'etre.

The task is also a difficult one, because we have learned in the
last fifteen years of scholarship that the Anabaptist movement in the
sixteenth century was a diverse movement with several points of
origin. Perhaps we should say that it was a series of movements.
Klaassen noted three separate, major points of origin: Switzerland,
South Germany, and the Netherlands. The diversity of the movement makes it difficult to know what to appropriate.

A second difficulty of the task is knowing how to appropriate
the past. Our situations differ. Paraphrasing what Klaassen said
concerning Harold S. Bender, "We are not sixteenth-century
Anabaptists, and the year is 1990, not 1525." Even when we know
the story, it is something else to know how to make use of that story.

Klaassen has given us a good statement on the use of that story.
He does not suggest that we imitate the story, in contrast to the earlier generation which was going to "recover the Anabaptist vision."
Klaassen suggests that it does provide some guidelines. The story
suggests an orientation toward the world, an orientation we can live
by.

By way of follow up, I have several conversation points about
some of Klaassen's interpretations of the story. These points deal
both with how we appropriate the sixteenth-century story, and how
we might want to examine the influence of the story in our ongoing
research.

1) I want to stress and affirm the fact that Klaassen did not use
the fact of a pluralistic sixteenth-century movement to rationalize
modern pluralism. On the contrary, Klaassen described a core of

ideas which was recognized in one form already by Harold Bender. With the new scholarship, we see that that core of ideas had other forms, and that not all Anabaptists reflected that core of ideas. Nonetheless, as Klaassen points out, there is a multi-faceted core of ideas that we can use in forms relevant to our context. The pluralism of sixteenth-century Anabaptism is neither the cause of nor the rationalization for modern pluralism.

2) My second point concerns history as a medium of revelation. I want to make sure we heard a very important theological point Klaassen made about history as revelatory. I agree that all parts of the sixteenth-century story are important, and that we learn from all of it, sometimes positively and sometimes negatively. However, the point I want to make is that all aspects of the story are not equal; all parts of the story are not applicable to our situation in the same way. When we identify ourselves as "Christian" (making ourselves part of a story which begins with Jesus), we are identifying a set of criteria by which to evaluate the sixteenth-century story and to distinguish the positive aspects from the negative.

In other words, to say that history is revelatory is not a rationalization of "what is." The gospel, the good news about Jesus of Nazareth, gives us an understanding, a grid, by which to measure what history reveals.

The next several points deal more specifically with what history reveals.

3) Klaassen stated first, and thus apparently of most prominence, that sixteenth-century Anabaptism had what he called an "ecumenical theology." In other words, they accepted the "basic theological affirmation of the ancient church," namely the Apostles' Creed, trinitarianism, the Nicene formula, and not mentioned explicitly by Klaassen, the Chalcedonian formula.

Klaassen is correct that sixteenth-century Anabaptists used these formulas. However, in spite of what Klaassen said about their acceptance of this ecumenical theology, I believe that there is another dimension to the discussion. It is also significant to point out how or why Anabaptists differed in their discussion of these issues. For example, take the "somewhat docetic christology" of Menno Simons and Dutch Anabaptism, to which Klaassen alluded. Although Menno indeed used trinitarian language, he nonetheless had a non-traditional christology. And that "somewhat docetic" (Klaassen's term) christological formulation was prompted in part because there were impulses shaping Menno that were not operating in the magisterial reformers. He wanted to describe a pure, visible church which took the life and teaching of Jesus as normative for Christians and thus a church which was distinguished from the world by its ethics. That impulse meant that in spite of Menno's use of the traditional trinitarian language and the traditional orthodox language of humanity and deity, there was an Anabaptist cast to it; there were ecclesiological and ethical dimensions not present for the magisterial reformation. I could make similar observations about other sixteenth-century Anabaptists, such as Hans Denck and Pilgram Marpeck, who used trinitarian language, but whose identity with Anabaptism also gave their use of the creedal language a different tone than that of the magisterial reformers.

Historically, Anabaptists did share the classic creeds, but assumptions they did not share with the magisterial reformers--discipleship, visible church, nonresistance, and more--can and often did put an Anabaptist cast on those classic formulations. I hope we do not get so interested in affirming our common heritage with mainline Christianity that we forget that it is these other dimensions which give us our way of reading the Bible. As Klaassen said, "What we cling to in our tradition is basically a certain way of interpreting the biblical evidence relating to our faith." The Bible and the early creeds look different depending on whether the reader assumes (such code words as) discipleship or the normativity of Jesus for ethics and a visible church. These Anabaptist assumptions are not recognized if we only emphasize that Anabaptists accepted the early creedal definitions.

Perhaps we are at a juncture where our context and discussion partners dictate whether to emphasize either that Anabaptists shared the creeds or had some additional perspectives and assumptions on that ecumenical theology. With reference to the dialectical trends charted by the editors (see page 9), e.g. the "Anabaptism-civic church" continuum, emphasizing Anabaptists' use of the orthodox, ecumenical definitions moves us toward the civic end of the continuum, while stressing the unique Anabaptist perspectives on those definitions moves us to the Anabaptist end of the continuum. I believe that in the late twentieth-century in North America, where we are concerned about assimilation and loss of identity, we need to focus more on the Anabaptist revisions than on the shared definitions.

4) Klaassen noted that transcendent anchorage is absolutely essential today. That is true, but a vital part of the discussion concerns the way to discuss the transcendent. Just because sixteenth-century Anabaptists quoted fourth and fifth century language does not mean that we need to use that same language to discuss transcendence. I would suggest that Norman Kraus's book on christology has given us a good start on discussing transcendence in terms of meta-history rather than meta-physics.

It is difficult to know how to measure these particular theological issues or even talk about them. The language that congregations understand do not quite cover these issues and theological transformation, and scholars might not agree with any of the language used to pose the theological identity questions. If we do not feel comfortable with any of the theological questions, perhaps I have just come up with a new way to be part of the time-honored Mennonite tradition of wanting to be "neither fundamentalist nor liberal."

5) On conversion, baptism, and sanctification of life I would simply say that conversion is not unique to Anabaptists and by itself does not tell us much. The crucial thing is to link it to sanctification. In other words, salvation is not just removal of guilt, but it is transformation to a changed life.

Unique to Anabaptists was not that they talked about conversion, or about Jesus. They were unique in their linkage so that the teaching and life of Jesus were a norm against which they attempted to measure their own lives. That linking (an outlook or attitude) is what we need to focus on in our research.

6) I have a similar comment concerning the church of believers. In my opinion, one of the most crucial things to learn from sixteenth-century Anabaptism is that the church is distinct from the world. The church is a sign and a witness to the world that the kingdom of God is different from the world. The church lives with the goal of transforming all of society into the kingdom of God, while living in full awareness of the reality that the church will do no more than be a witness to the final transformation which will be culminated by the return of Christ. As Klaassen said, sixteenth-century Anabaptists repudiated the church as territorial, they rejected princely/ducal jurisdiction of church, they challenged economic arrangements, and rejected the sword and official violence. Those same concerns appear in other forms today, but the principle of the church being distinct from the world is still valid.

7) The church as distinct from the world is, I believe, the proper context in which to understand the concept of *sola scripture*. Again, the Bible is something which belongs to all Christians. Every Christian, of whatever tradition, can or does own a Bible. What distinguished Anabaptists was not the fact they owned Bibles or read them. The distinguishing mark was the way they read the Bible, assuming that the life and teaching of Jesus and the apostles which they found in the Bible was *normative* for their lives. That is the same assumption which makes the church distinct from the world today and which gives a potential Anabaptist cast to our use of the creedal definitions of the early church councils.

For me, the distinguishing marks of Anabaptism can all be

organized under the rubric of the church distinguished from the world. Ultimately that is a christological statement; it is different because the church is founded on Christ. The scriptures which tell the story of Jesus are the most direct source for this foundation. Since it is different from the world, all members are visible, and thus every member is inherently a witness. Thus it is quite appropriate that people share in leadership roles. The church exists by the grace of God. Given the seemingly overwhelming forces arranged against us, it takes faith to say that it indeed represents God in history. Baptism marks one's entry into that story and it also marks one's acceptance of the grace of God active in that story.

What Klaassen and I have described is an idealized statement of the believers' church. It is a goal toward which we strive more than something which already exists. What we want to discover in our research is the extent to which this model or vision is an integrating factor of modern Mennonite identity.

CHAPTER 2

SHIFTING MENNONITE THEOLOGICAL ORIENTATIONS

C. Norman Kraus

Since the first Church Member Profile questionnaire was prepared,[1] significant shifts in the social and theological climate have changed not only the configuration of our church patterns but also the way Mennonites currently think about doctrine and ethics. In order to appreciate these changes we first need to briefly survey the background of the first questionnaire and the changing scene since then. Then we need to assess trends in the religious climate which provide the backdrop for theological thinking today. Last, I will explore what the new questions for theological reconstruction are today.

SURVEY OF THE MENNONITE SCENE 1900-1988

In the first half of this present century, denominationalism still provided the religious parameters for the definition of religious groups, and Mennonites were struggling to find their self-identity in this context. They were shedding their sectarian skin for a larger more comfortable denominational one. This meant, among other things, that the different Mennonite groups self-consciously attempted to define and organize their own denominational identities vis-a-vis one another. Thus we cannot tell one unified story of development; but as Pannabecker observes, "the problems of the times were faced by all Mennonites" (1968), and reactions were similar. For our purposes the focus will be on those problems and their impact upon Mennonites.

In their attempt to cope with the dynamic changes which were transpiring around them and sucking them into the larger religious vortex, Mennonites, on the one hand, tried to shore up their inherited tradition with new exhortatory literature and appeals to Menno and the Anabaptist ancestors. On the other, they turned to the revivalist movement, especially via Moody and Moody Bible Institute, for renewal patterns and techniques.

Theologically they tended to associate with the Reformed tradition rather than the Lutheran. They preferred its Arminian wing although they did not identify denominationally with its various organizational expressions (Free Methodists, Free Will Baptists, Nazarenes). The denominations were still part of the "English" religious world. However, a clue to Mennonite biases may be found in the choice of seminaries by young scholars. Baptist and Presbyterian institutions predominated up to 1950.

An interesting example of the proliferation of voices which were influencing Mennonite doctrine may be cited from the 1914 preface of *Christian Doctrine* edited by Daniel Kauffman. The book which covers the whole range of theological doctrine from God and creation to the "Future Destiny of Man" was written by a symposium of authors with quite different theological training. Kauffman wrote in the preface,"...the following are among the authors and works consulted: *What the Bible Teaches*--Torrey; *Systematic Theologies*--Clarke, Brown, Hodge, Wakefield, Evans, Strong; *Encyclopedias*--Schaff-Herzog, Britannica, Inglis, etc.; *Public Worship*--Pattison; *Theopneustia*--Gaussen; *Ecclesiology*--Johnson; *The World and its God*--Mauro; *Wahres Christendum*--Arndt; *People's Bible*--Parker."

What is so striking about this list is its variation. Calvinist and Arminian, Fundamentalist and liberal, denominational and nondenominational, premillennial and nonmillennial, all have a reading! In its later edition (1928) Kauffman attempted to pull together a Mennonite synthesis which had wide influence among Mennonites, and for a generation defined Mennonite doctrine for many.

During this period doctrinal beliefs were discussed under the familiar labels of Calvinism-Arminianism, pre-, post-, and nonmillennialism, Scofield dispensationalism, biblical infallibility and authority, liberal and conservative theology, nonresistance and nonconformity, mode and proper time of baptism, close communion, etc. Ethical issues were still largely defined in terms of the community tradition.

But the new influences of Pentecostalism and fundamentalism were also impacting the churches and even causing divisions. Pentecostalism was generally rejected and relegated to the polemical fringes. Increasingly fundamentalism and its issues dominated the attention of the church leaders. These issues clustered around the inerrancy and literal interpretation of the Bible--issues such as literal creation, virgin birth, physical resurrection, and literal and premillennial second coming of Christ.[2]

We should probably add that theological liberalism with its

rationalistic assumptions had relatively little affect upon Mennonites of this period. Insofar as it rejected the older Calvinistic scholasticism and appealed to a reasonable and historical interpretation of Scripture, Liberalism did make its impression on a few Mennonite scholars. But their position would be more correctly described as a modified conservatism than modernism or liberalism (cf. Pannabecker, 1968:221).

This brings us to roughly the second half of this century--the years following the Second World War. Fundamentalism and Modernism had pretty well fought to a draw, although not a tie. The mainline denominations had settled for neoorthodox or moderately liberal theological positions, and the initiative was with the ecumenical movement and the emerging "neoliberalism" and "biblical realism." Then rather unexpectedly a neofundamentalism which labelled itself "evangelicalism" emerged from the old fundamentalist circles. Scholars from the fundamentalist camp were admitting that changes needed to be made, but what kind of changes?

This was the period when these newer more moderate and biblical positions were being introduced into our Mennonite seminaries. The "inductive method of Bible study" which involved the cautious use of the methodology and conclusions of biblical criticism gradually undercut the inerrancy theory of biblical inspiration. Acceptance of modern theories concerning the age and evolutionary development of the earth (not, I might add, its origin) resurrected the fears of those who were comfortable with fundamentalist positions. The introduction of "Anabaptism" as a more biblical alternative to Protestant Fundamentalism, and the energetic expansion of Christian social service as an authentic expression of the gospel shifted the issues and heightened the tension. This was a dynamic but tense period in our colleges and seminaries. It was a period in which theologically trained leadership and the laity moved further apart at least temporarily.

Reflecting this dynamic change, the Mennonite Church (MC) adopted a new confession of faith in 1963. It was in the best of the conservative tradition, but it made stragetic changes in wording which clearly reversed emphases of the 1921 "Fundamentals of the Faith" statement. It modified the position on the seven "ordinances," bringing them more into line with other Mennonite groups. It emphasized the "equality" of men and women, and defined the difference between them as "functional." It left out the technical term of "inerrancy" and limited the Bible's infallible authority to its spiritual and moral guidance. It gave new prominence to "love and nonresistance," and relieved nonconformity of its legalistic character.

It was soon clear that this statement reflected a conservative response to the radical changes taking place among Mennonites. The late 60s and early 70s ushered in a period of radical social change in America, and Mennonites were strongly impacted by it. Both mores and morals, doctrine and ecclesiastic organization, biblical interpretation and practice were deeply affected. These would include attitudes toward politics, virtual rejection of traditional positions on modesty and "moral purity," changing attitude toward beverage alcohol, substantial changes in sexual mores and practice, general acceptance of the capitalistic business ethic, changes in women's social roles, and the like.

For many who were caught in this revolutionary situation the trauma was compounded by the fact that from the old perspectives no satisfactory biblical rationale was forthcoming to justify the changes. The traditional values had been based directly and often literally on an infallible biblical text. Thus change in practice raised the question why the interpretation of the Bible suddenly had changed, or why the Bible no longer had authority for us. Seen from this perspective all these changes are theological in character, and the radical shift suggests a movement toward secularism. This change had begun before and was one of the reasons for gathering new information on what was happening to Mennonites (Kauffman and Harder, 1975).

Indications are that pluralism of opinion and practice continues to grow. Small groups in favor of little or no change have formed to rescue the church from apostasy (e.g., the Fellowship of Concerned Mennonites). At the opposite end, hopefully also a small group, are those who continue to leave the churches because of dissatisfaction with its positions. Indicators like the "Young Adult Profile" research project conducted by the General Conference and Mennonite Mission Boards seem to tell us that among the "silent majority" opinions continue to diversify.[3]

THEOLOGICAL TRENDS INFLUENCING MENNONITE ATTITUDES

The basic patterns of theological alignment today remain what they were in the early 1970s (ecumenical and evangelical, orthodox/fundamentalist and liberal, Roman Catholic, Protestant, and Anabaptist), but the shifting mood and issues are important and need to be researched. Movements like liberation theology, feminist theology, Pentecostal/charismatic renewal, and fundamentalism itself have made significant new strides in the last decade or two.

Perhaps the most obvious development on the theological scene is the increased pluralism and eclecticism which makes it diffi-

cult to easily categorize positions. This is evidenced by diversifica-
tion of opinion within movements as well as by the creation of new
movements. This is an evangelical as well as an ecumenical (liberal)
phenomenon.

The Evangelical Scene

In 1970 evangelicalism was still fairly unified although cracks
were beginning to appear. *Newsweek* declared 1976 "the year of the
evangelical." But Fuller Theological Seminary was steadily pushing
for a more open and non-separatist theological position, and by 1978
public challenge and debate erupted in the so-called "battle for the
Bible" (Marsden, 1987:252ff). While evangelicalism has maintained
its ascendecy on the church scene, it has splintered into a variety of
theological emphases--at least the variety has become much more
obvious. This development has gone so far that some are beginning
to speak of a "post-evangelical" era just as ecumenicals speak of a
"post-liberal" era.[4]

Evangelicalism and Fundamentalism

This diversity has become most obvious in the fundamentalist
schism within evangelicalism itself. The evangelical movement
began as a neo-fundamentalism determined to keep and give more
depth to the basic theological position of fundamentalism, to update
its social conscience, but to relax its separatist and nonpolitical
stance.[5] Under the banner of evangelism, with the Billy Graham
organization as its agent and the Fuller Theological Seminary as its
new academic champion, it formed a coalition of conservative and
fundamentalist forces in the National Association of Evangelicals.
The fundamentalism of old stalwarts like John R. Rice, Bob Jones,
and Carl McIntire was to be superseded by a more reasonable and
tolerant evangelicalism.

In the early 1970s this movement looked so strong that the
authors of *Anabaptism Four Centuries Later* thought that fundamentalism had "largely spent itself" (1975:109). As a matter of fact quite
the opposite has happened. Fundamentalism has recouped,
reorganized, and clearly defined itself as a movement over against
evangelicalism. The formation in 1978 of the International Council
on Biblical Inerrancy by Harold Lindsell, Kenneth Kantzer and
others was a clear signal to the more conservative forces. Lindsell
was no longer willing to be tagged "evangelical." By 1982 Jerry Falwell (1981) and his followers were ready to openly break with
evangelicals who were soft on biblical inerrancy and the political

concerns of his "Moral Majority."
The distinctive characteristics of this new fundamentalism[6] are biblical literalism and inerrancy, rightist political convictions and activity, and the championing of a "Christian America." Of course they continue to emphasize the "new birth" and personal morality, and the fundamentals of "old time religion." But here again it is difficult to make generalizations about the movement because of the diversity within it. Advocates as different as Jerry Falwell, Pat Robertson, and Harold Lindsell, and a host of televangelists like Oral Roberts and Jimmy Swaggart belong loosely to this right wing of evangelicalism.

Christian "Reconstructionism"

One of the groups that fits into this category are the "Christian Reconstructionists" who advocate that America return to its ideal as a Christian republic under the rule of biblical law. They hold that God entered into a covenant with America through its founding fathers to be his representative nation, and the nation will lose its blessings of wealth and freedom if it does not "reconstruct" its sociopolitical order according to this pattern. While Pat Robertson was not one of the founders of the movement, his recent book *The Secret Kingdom* (1982) suggest this possibility.[7]
I mention these rightist movements because there is clear indication of their influence upon conservative groups in the Mennonite denominations. The publications of the Fellowship of Concerned Mennonites along with *Guidelines for Today* and *Sword and Trumpet* all take a fundamentalistic position on numerous issues and appeal to these leaders to support their positions.

Pentecostal-Charismatic

Another group within the more conservative wing of evangelicalism is the Pentecostal-charismatic collage. Here again the diversity within the movement almost defies categorization. Basically charismatics are fundamentalistic in theological method and doctrine, but not separatist and bellicose in spirit. Indeed, renewal and unity of spiritual experience characterize its mood.
The charismatic movement is not strictly speaking a theological movement, but its emphasis on a special experience of "Holy Spirit baptism and speaking in tongues" promotes the Pentecostal theology. On the one hand its emphasis on experience rather than rational thought de-emphasizes the significance of overt theology.

But on the other, its strong insistence on a unique experience of the
Holy Spirit highlights a distinctive theological view which is usually
attached to a fundamentalistic structure. Its religious mood and
political stance can be as different as the movements led by Pat
Robertson and Jimmy Swaggart.

Again, this movement has had a powerful impact upon the
Mennonite churches. It has influenced the shape of worship. It has
provided a route to personal spiritual renewal and Christian
tolerance. But it has also led to division, and it has underscored the
fundamentalist themes for others who accepted the more stringent
Pentecostal separatist doctrines of Holy Spirit baptism.

Church Growth

Yet another movement which has had a significant practical
impact on the theological emphases in our churches is Church
Growth. At its inception the movement sought to go beyond the
concept of salvation as a purely private spiritual transaction involving
individuals only. It focused upon "people groups" within which individuals identified themselves as the objects of conversion. The
objective of evangelism and mission is to plant churches and not just
to save individuals.

As the movement has developed it has become pragmatic and
technique oriented. While the theological convictions of its main
advocates were evangelical, it claims to be a sociological method
which can be used by churches of any theological orientation to produce growth in membership.

This emphasis upon technique and accomplishment of goals
has had subtle but very real implications for evangelical theology. It
has encouraged activism and the idea that the salvation of human
kind is quite dependent upon the efforts of the church--an anti-
Calvinist bias. With its sharp division between "evangelizing" and
"discipling," it has defined the theology of salvation in minimal terms.
The evangelist is not making disciples but merely eliciting a response
to the Savior from a particular social class or people group. In
cross-cultural outreach this has led to the advocacy of a very free
contextualization of the message of the gospel. All of this has
caused a great deal of tension within the larger evangelical movement.

The Church Growth movement has clearly impacted the Mennonite denominations. On the one hand, its emphasis on church fellowship rather than the lone individual appealed to the Anabaptist
bias. And its emphasis on active church development is a welcome
one. On the other hand, one suspects that it has increased the

theological priority of "evangelism" as opposed to "discipling" and nurturing. If so, it would likely mean that conservative Protestant concepts of salvation have been reinforced and the importance of distinctively Mennonite theological emphases undercut. It would be good to have some confirmation or refutation of this.

Relational Models

I have emphasized the pluralism in the evangelical movement, but perhaps we can get some overall perspective on the movement in the following diagram.

Conservative Protestantism (Evangelicals)

Conservatives
(Denominationalism)

Fundamentalists
(Nondenominationalism)

Neo-Fundamentalists

Neo-Evangelicals

Radical Evangelicals

As the diagram suggests the movement within evangelicalism has been back toward a centrist position within conservative Protestant denominationalism (a non-separatist position). Neo-fundamentalists are less concerned about the churchly traditions and define true Christianity as a basic orthodox belief system ("the fundamentals"). Those who hold to such beliefs belong to the true church. They still tend to withdraw from fellowship with those who do not agree.

The Neo-evangelicals, in the words of George Marsden, "cultivated a positive evangelicalism, open to almost any trend or movement that did not involve overt heresy" (1987:266). Heresy was defined as clear deviation from the Nicea-Chalcedonian tradition. They consciously sought to move into the mainstream of conservative denominationalism.

The radical evangelicals include a variety of positions which have been more influenced by contemporary social concerns, anthropological understanding of culture and language, existentialist correction to rationalist philosophy, and Anabaptist concern for the centrality of Jesus and discipleship. Nevertheless they continue to find their self-identity in the non-liberal circles by deliberate choice. They affirm the unique personal reality of God's self-revelation in Jesus Christ as it is recorded in Scripture. Thus Scripture continues to have normative authority for them across cultural relativities.

During this same period there are indications that Mennonites have also become more pluralistic and tolerant of differences in theology and religious experience. Increased inter-Mennonite dialogue and cooperation, acceptance of charismatics within the fellowship, beginnings of inter-denominational dialogue, the organization of fundamentalist oriented groups within the denominational structures, the pervasive use of historical-critical Bible study methods in our academic institutions, and the espousal of philosophical positions like Process Thought in articles appearing in Mennonite publications all point toward increased pluralism and tolerance. How far these developments reflect a broad base of change, and how far they are the product of an elite corps of organizational leaders is not entirely clear. Has theological opinion really changed significantly at the grassroots?

The dynamic plurality within Mennonitism parallels that of the evangelical movement as a whole, and the relationship of the two movements might be diagrammed on a parallel continuum as follows (reading from right to left).

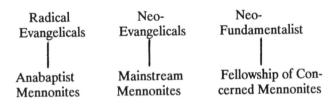

Radical Evangelicals	Neo- Evangelicals	Neo- Fundamentalist
Anabaptist Mennonites	Mainstream Mennonites	Fellowship of Con- cerned Mennonites

The Ecumenical (Liberal) Scene

Liberalism, now often referred to as ecumenicalism in contrast to evangelicalism, has always been pluralistic by its very nature. Earlier in this century a "modernist" version which made empiricism the final arbiter of religious truth was dominant. Today this optimistic modernism with its faith in science is largely outmoded. Liberalism, or rather liberalisms, are in a "post-modern" mode. Such liberalism remains strong in academic circles, but it has suffered great setbacks in mainline denominations. Both the National Council of Churches and the World Council of Churches have declined during the past two decades. And the mainline, liberally-inclined denominations have lost membership and political influence.

Post-modern liberalism has not forsaken the basic premise that human experience is limited to the empirical realm, but it has refined and extended its definition of the empirical. Under the influence of logical and linguistic analysis it has revised its methodology and use of language and argued that a basic belief posture ("blik") is necessary in the empirical process. In this way it makes space for the importance and rationality of religious conviction. Thus the dominant mood of post-modern liberalism is not agnosticism but relativism.

Contemporary liberalism is pluralistic by conviction and design. It is much less tied to one particular ideology than the earlier modernism. It is oriented to the human scene and very conscious of the relativity of human culture. It defines religion in terms of human values rather than theological verities, and it is ready to contextualize its "truth" statements.

This relativistic stance has significant implications for understanding the authority of the Bible for the church. Liberal scholars are very conscious of both the Bible's cultural origins and limitations, and of the present day interpreters' contextual conditioning. Thus modern interpretations of Scripture are strictly relative to the interpreter's situation and competence, and the Bible cannot be a unifying authority for the church universal except for the barest historical information.

This cultural relativising of biblical authority in turn affects the understanding of Jesus' role as the universal Savior of humankind. Jesus, like the Bible, was the product of his own historical culture. That in itself does not deny that he was an authentic revelation of God to his own culture, but it raises the question of his authoritative relationship to other cultures. He is the progenitor of the Christian church and can be the Savior of those who choose to stand in that religious tradition. He is a unique but not the only Savior of humankind. Thus the authority and saviorhood of Jesus as the Son of God is relativised.[8]

The more strident voices of the late 1960s advocating a "secular Christianity" have quieted down, but historicism and empiricism remain basic assumptions for humanistic religious liberalism. At the lay level more relativism, theological eclecticism, a general disregard for biblical authority, and belief that there are many ways to God are indications of this spirit. Mennonite scholars are confronted with this kind of thinking in the universities, and clearly the laity is being influenced by this kind of thinking more than in the past.

Liberation Theology

The past quarter century has also seen the rise of several other theological movements within ecumenical Christianity. Liberation theology, first as "Black" theology and then in its Hispanic version, has made an impact. This movement has cut across Roman Catholic and Protestant lines, and there are both liberal and evangelical versions of it.

Liberation theology begins with the assumption that the Bible must be read in the context of the poor and oppressed as a message of liberation. The historical Jesus must be understood as the friend and liberator of the poor. Theology must confess a God who gives himself to and for the downtrodden. It should not begin with abstract definitions of God and his relation to the world, but with God as he is present in the midst of suffering and death to heal, redeem, and create shalom.

Some in this movement have based their theology on a Marxist analysis of the plight of the poor and have given the gospel a political revolutionary cast. But the major contribution of the movement seems to have been its awakening of a new social sensitivity in biblical studies. And its predominant impact seems to have been its challenge to the church to take its social responsibility more seriously as an integral part of the gospel.

Mennonites have probably been more influenced by its evangelical version represented by persons like Samuel Escobar, Rene Padilla, and Orlando Costas. Their version is much nearer to our Mennonite emphasis on service and nonviolent social action. Even so it is a more radical hands-on approach to social action than Mennonites have traditionally espoused. It would be interesting to know whether and how much the more radical thought of liberation theology has changed Mennonite thinking.

Feminist Theology

Feminist theology is one of the "liberation" theologies that has become a distinct movement in itself. The feminist theologians range from the radically liberal, who reject the authority of the Bible as the product of chauvinistic patriarchy and doubt that salvation by a male savior is possible, to the warmly evangelical, who struggle with the seeming contradictions of the New Testament teachings on the subject but highlight the gospel's affirmation of equality.

There is no question that this emphasis has had a strong impact on Mennonites, but it will be interesting to see just how far it has penetrated. How aware are they of the issues? Have Mennonites in general joined with the position of Bill Gothard and "Fascinating Womanhood Foundation" or the evangelical feminists or the more radical/liberal feminists? Are there any distinct emphases that characterize Mennonite feminists?

Roman Catholicism

The changed situation in the relation and dialogue between Roman Catholic and Protestant theology also requires notice. Roman Catholic writers and themes, especially the more liberal ones, are much more influential in Protestant circles than they were twenty five years ago. Names like Rahner, Küng, Dulles, Sobrino are well known in our seminaries. However there is some question in my mind concerning the importance of questions in this area. It is doubtful that Mennonite believers in general are aware of these authors or the theological dialogues taking place. It might, however, be of interest to determine whether attitudes toward Catholicism have changed.

NEW AREAS TO BE PROBED

The Kauffman and Harder (1975) study followed the pattern of questions used by Glock and Stark in order to have a basis of comparison with denominational Protestantism. This is quite understandable and helpful, but the pluralism of our situation demands more specificity in the "belief" questions in order to determine more clearly the theological identification of Mennonites. Where do our people stand on the orthodox liberal continuum and how much have they been influenced by the onslaught of the religious mass media?

In several areas we need to sharpen the focus of our inquiry. Specifically, we need to be more precise in the distinctions between fundamentalism and orthodoxy. Does the high degree of orthodoxy in Mennonite answers indicate fundamentalist influence and belief patterns? Or does it merely indicate continuing agreement with traditional denominational Protestant theological patterns? This kind of distinction may be difficult to detect, but I think that it can be done. John Yoder is right when he points out that the use of beliefs to exclude people from fellowship is a distinguishing characteristic of Fundamentalism (Kauffman and Harder, 1975:114).

In Fundamentalism the word "fundamental" means necessary to the definition of "Christian." This conviction leads fundamentalists to maximize distinctions by emphasizing certain key words and phrases--shibboleths or flash words, if you please. This is such an endemic and consistent characteristic that we can use it to distinguish between a fundamentalist position and a more conventional conservative view with a high degree of confidence.[9]

Further, we need to discern the extent of liberal penetration into Mennonite circles. It is not enough to take negative evidence, i.e., not believing orthodox statements, in order to determine degrees of liberalism. Attitudes toward the exclusive claims of Christianity--especially the unique claim of Jesus as Savior--opinions about "myths" in the Bible, beliefs about the supernatural could be used as indicators.

As we have seen in the second section of the papers, there are a number of new theological trends which have had considerable impact on the churches over the past twenty-five years. These require additional research. Certainly, for example, we should examine the impact of feminism from a variety of perspectives, both social and theological.

The extent of the charismatic movement's influence should be tested. Belief patterns, attitudes toward the significance of theology as an intellectual discipline, and attitudes toward self-fulfillment, wealth as a blessing from God, as well as "religious experience" should be probed. The necessity or desirability of "baptism in the Spirit and speaking in tongues" lies at the heart of the movement. One of the more radical wings of the movement advocates that God wants his children to be healthy and prosperous materially as well as spiritually. God has blessed North America with wealth because it has honored him. The negative of this is that disease (e.g. AIDS) and suffering (e.g. poverty) are the direct judgment of God. There are evidences that this teaching has had an impact, but how widespread is it?

Also the charismatic movement has broken with traditional orthodoxy on the question of miracles. They insist that miracles continue to happen and that we should pray for and expect miracles in our daily life. One suspects from everyday usage in Mennonite circles that most lay people think of miracles simply as unusual fortunate coincidences in life which they attribute to God.

Beliefs and attitudes of our members about missions need investigation. We know that the number of overseas missionaries from Mennonite churches has declined steadily over the past twenty-five years. Does this indicate a loss of conviction, or are there other explanations? What priorities do our members give evangelism, service, witness for peace, and justice, etc.? What is the perceived role of missionaries?

In a recent winter Bible school class of twenty-seven adults, which included several preachers, I surveyed their opinion about the current role of missionaries. Only three marked "saving souls from damnation" as their first or second priority! The most votes were cast for "preaching the gospel of the kingdom," and next in priority was "being present as the ambassadors of Christ." This was a select group of people interested in missions. Would these people make a difference between cross-cultural mission and "evangelism and church growth" at home? What is the general opinion?

One of the interesting developments in Fundamentalism is its alliance with right wing politics and its championing of an evangelical civil religion. Indeed, this has become a hallmark of the aggressive champions of the movement, e.g., Falwell. Further examples are Pat Robertson's assertion that America has a divine destiny, the claim that the vision of the "Founding Fathers" was Christian, and that through a great spiritual and moral revival we must return to their vision and defeat the secularism and humanism that are engulfing our political process. We must "vote on the moral issues" in national elections. Our children must regain the right of prayer and religious teaching in the public schools. We must outlaw abortion, etc.

Such thinking, of course, challenges Mennonite concepts of the separation of church and state, but there is evidence of a softening on this issue among some of the more fundamentalistically inclined leaders. I suggest that this is an important area for more investigation.

And finally, with the advent of "Christian" television and radio stations we probably need to give more attention to the listening and watching habits of our constituents. From whom are they taking their clues? Oral and Richard Roberts? Pat Robertson? Robert Schuller? Jerry Falwell? John Wimber? Kenneth and Gloria Coplin? Charles and Francis Hunter? Billy Graham? Jimmy Swaggart? Others? And how regularly do they listen to these programs? It would also be of great interest to know how the recent tele-evangelist scandals have affected the Mennonite viewing audience.

The Mennonite denominations are in a dynamic social flux at this time. Will Mennonites simply adapt and be absorbed into the general patterns of American evangelical religion? Or will they be able to recoup and hold to the distinctive witness of their Anabaptist heritage?

NOTES

1 "Church Member Profile, A Study of Members in Five Denominations," Questionnaire prepared by J. Howard Kauffman and Leland Harder, no date, but administered in 1972. The results were reported in *Anabaptists Four Centuries Later, A profile of Five Mennonite and Brethren In Christ Denominations,* Herald Press, 1975.

2 Beulah Stauffer Hostetler has given us an insightful interpretative analysis of the impact of these influences on the Franconia Mennonites in her *American Mennonites and Protestant Movements*, (Scottdale: Herald Press, 1987). Theron Schlabach also wrestles with some of these issues in *Gospel Versus Gospel: Mission and the Mennonite Church, 1863-1944,* (Scottdale: Herald Press, 1980), and in his more recent work, *Peace, Faith, Nation: Mennonites and Amish in Nineteenth-Century America* (1988).

3 See SYAS/COE study project, part II, published by Mennonite Board of Missions and Commission on Education, Elkhart, IN and Newton, KS, 1986.

4 Denominational theological emphases have begun to reassert themselves as valid "evangelical" traditions. Fuller Theological Seminary has completed its "reform of Fundamentalism" (George Marsden, *Reforming Fundamentalism*, Grand Rapids: Eerdmans, 1987) and moved into a next stage of the evangelical mid-stream. It is now attempting to serve these traditions. Ron Sider has pushed the conscience of fundamentalism far beyond anything C. F. H. Henry anticipated. Clark Pinnock has forsaken the ranks of Lindsell's biblical inerrantists. The Church Growth advocates have developed a pragmatic program which is quite eclectic in its theology and designed to help any church add new members. And Bernard Ramm, long one of the staunch defenders of a more fundamentalistic evangelicalism, has written *After Fundamentalism, the Future of Evangelical Theology* (1983) in which he gives Karl Barth an appreciative reevaluation. We seem to have passed an era!

5 This was the basic distinction which I used in 1978 when I diagramed the "Ideological Umbrellas" under which the various evangelical movements were clustered. See "The Great Evangelical Coalition," in *Evangelicalism and Anabaptism* (Scottdale: Herald Press, 1979, p. 40).

6 This must be called "new fundamentalism" because it too has repudiated the older non-political and strictly separatist stance. Advocates of the older movement still exist and have disclaimed Falwell's leadership.

7 The movement began with Cornelius Van Til who taught at Westminster Theological Seminary. It is clearly postmillennialist in the old Calvinist tradition, but it has taken on a right wing fundamentalist identity. It seems to have been part of Pat Robertson's motivation to enter the political arena for the 1988 elections. In part II of *The Secret Kingdom* (Nashville: Thomas Nelson, 1982), Robertson outlines "The Laws of the Kingdom" which even now secretly control social, economic, and political relationships. But although he gives many biblical references, the political picture that emerges fits the conservative capitalistic, military ideal of fundamentalist Christians. See also "The Reconstructionist Movement on the New Christian Right"

(*Christian Century*, October 4, 1989, 880-82).

8 This position has been clearly described in the symposium edited by John Hick and Paul F. Knitter, *The Myth of Christian Uniqueness, Toward a Pluralistic Theology of Religions* (Maryknoll, New York:Orbis, 1987). While there are different positions expounded in the symposium, the basic position is that "the myth of God incarnate" is one myth among many religious myths, and Christianity should be in dialogue with these other religious traditions rather than try to convert them to the exclusive claims of Jesus.

9 Following are a list of examples that could be used: inerrancy rather than infallible, substitutionary (atonement) rather than vicarious, "the blood" rather than cross of Christ, *literal* and premillenial second coming rather than more vague statements, virgin born Son of God rather than simply virgin birth, supernatural new birth, and *physical* resurrection of Christ.

REFERENCES

Falwell, Jerry, (Ed.)
1981 *The Fundamentalist Phenomenon*. Garden City: Doubleday.

Hick, John and Paul Knitter, (Eds.)
1987 *The Myth of Christian Uniqueness, Toward a Pluralistic Theology of Religions*. Maryknoll, NY.:Orbis.

Hostetler, Beulah
1987 *Mennonites and Protestant Movements*. Scottdale: Herald Press.

Kauffman, Daniel, (Ed.)
1914 *Bible Doctrine*. Scottdale: Mennonite Publishing House.

Kauffman, Howard and Leland Harder
1975 *Anabaptism Four Centuries Later*. Scottdale: Herald Press.

Kraus, C. Norman, (Ed.)
1979 *Evangelicalism and Anabaptism*. Scottdale: Herald Press.

Lindsell, Harold
1976 *The Battle for the Bible*. Grand Rapids: Zondervan.

Marsden, George
1987 *Reforming Fundamentalism*. Grand Rapids: Eerdmans.

Pannabecker, Samuel F.
1968 *Faith in Ferment*. Newton, KS: Faith and Life.

Ramm, Bernard
1983 *After Fundamentalism, The Future of Evangelical Theology*. San Francisco: Harper and Row.

Robertson, Pat
1982 *The Secret Kingdom*. Nashville: Thomas Nelson.

Schlabach, Theron
   1980 *Gospel Versus Gospel: Mission and the Mennonite Church, 1863-1944.* Scottdale: Herald Press.

RESPONSE

Paul Toews

The task in which Norman and the rest of us are engaged in might be thought of as map-making. We are trying to determine what elements ought to go into the map that we are drawing to outline the shape of the Mennonite world. We are not actually at the stage of drawing the map. But we are determining what things to look for on the reconnoitor expedition. What we decide to look for of course will determine what we find and that in turn will shape the kind of map we draw.

We all know that maps are important when traveling in foreign terrain. There we are dependent upon the map. We miss what it does not include. But maps are also needed in familiar territory if we are looking for particularity. We can pass by something frequently and not see it till we have a map that names the place. Mapping is naming. By providing a name and some descripters, things previously hidden become visible. There is that suggestive line from Wallace Stevens that "we live in the description of a place and not in the place itself." Perhaps overstated, but indicative of the power of the descriptions that we do create.

My small part of this cartographical exercise in response to the Norman Kraus paper is to think a bit about theological geography. I wish to do so with two comments and two footnotes.

Two Comments

1. I began by thinking about the adequacy of the 1970s Church Member Profile I map for the 1990s. That map of the theological landscape included three differing theologies: General orthodoxy, Fundamentalist orthodoxy and Anabaptism (not Anabaptist orthodoxy which would have completed the parallelism). The map suggested a triangle with Mennonite theology oscillating (with denominational variation) between the three poles.

Trying to determine the adequacy of the 1970s map, I thought it might be interesting to check the interface between the theological beliefs of Mennonite individuals of the 1970s and today. Now of course not having the study replicated to check private belief against private belief, I was left with checking private belief against public dialogue.

My way of doing that was an arbitrary decision to do a hurried content analysis of the churchly periodicals of the three larger groups of the survey. I limited myself to an investigation of the *Gospel Herald, The Mennonite* and *The Christian Leader,* the MB publication for the US church. The *Gospel Herald* and *The Mennonite* purport to be bi-national. My unscientific sample was limited to January to June, 1987. And further, my sample was restricted to the lead article and the editorial. My intent was to try to determine to what extent the three theological systems referred to in the 1970s map still contain and inform Mennonite theologizing. One could argue from a variety of positions with the choice of 1987. Granting for the sake of discussion the reliability of the sample, we can say Orthodoxy is dead. What is alive is orthopraxis ideation. That is to say, the measures used in 1972 (Kauffman and Harder, 1975) to define both General Orthodoxy and Fundamentalist Orthodoxy are entirely missing from these six months of the churchly press. I found not one article dealing with the seven measures of General Orthodoxy or the seven measures of Fundamentalist Orthodoxy. Now I must hasten to add that the Anabaptist Orthodoxy measures did not fare much better. Of the eight measures identified in 1975, only two appeared in these six months--discipleship and non-resistance.

If the editors are in tune with their readers and reflect the theological habits of our people, then doctrines of God, miracles, a personal devil, and resurrection no longer need discussion. Doctrines of the virgin birth, creation, flood, eternal punishment have disappeared from our public discourse. Likewise concerns about oath-taking, litigation, baptism, and church discipline have faded.

If there is an overarching theme to these periodicals in 1987 it is that of the kingdom. That kingdom is often found in hidden places. The wisdom of the conventional has been replaced by the unexpected. The kingdom comes in the pregnant teenager who happens to be the mother of Jesus; in ordinary citizens who end up as radical disciples; and in disabled persons who mediate the loving and compassionate Father.

This search for the kingdom occurs within a psychological stance that rejects the mainstream. One author in the *Gospel Herald* best expressed this tilt with the concern "to be a little off center." The search for what it means to be "off center" is done in a series of categories that bear little relationship to those of Orthodoxy and Fundamentalism.

The denominational press, perhaps once dominated by doctrine, history, and missions, has given way to issues of social responsibility, service, spirituality, gender, sexuality, church growth, ethnicity, and pluralism. The style also seems different. The editorials are infrequently didactic and generally avuncular. The straight line logic of systematics has given way to circularity, irony, and paradox.

The point is not to suggest that General Orthodox and Fundamental Orthodox commitments are no longer part of Mennonite understanding, but rather that they seem to be peripheral to at least substantial parts of the Mennonite theological imagination. Measuring assent (which is probably still high) may not be revelatory for determining what activates Mennonite theologizing or praxis.

2. Norman Kraus's paper points us to the new map. There are many more places on the landscape. He highlights pluralism as the new reality that needs to be mapped. Already latent in the 1972 study, it has become the dominating theme.

The pluralist idiom, I think, gained entrance into Mennonite theological parlance only in the early 1980s. Today it has become one of our passwords. Witness the "Conference on Mennonite Pluralism" (1982); the "Conversations on Faith I and II" (1984 and 85); the "Dialogues on Faith I and II" (1984 and 85); the "Colloquium on Mennonite Systematic Theology" (1983); and the recent "Beyond Pluralism: What Mennonites Believe Today" conference (1988).

While we have been quick to pick up on the notion of pluralism, it seems to me that the predominate way Mennonites are playing the pluralism game is to point to the diversity of influences that are now circulating in our world and that represent alternatives to "Anabaptism." One example makes the point: A pastoral letter on spirituality from a Ministry of Spirituality Committee appointed by the MC General Board published in the May 5, 1987 *Gospel Herald* identified six streams of spirituality in the MC church:

> Anabaptist spirituality
> Conservative/Evangelical spirituality
> Relational spirituality
> Charismatic spirituality
> Feminist spirituality
> Contemplative spirituality

This approach to the question of pluralism tends to begin with the assumption of a unified Anabaptism and partially thinks of pluralism in terms of the more familiar Mennonite conceptual category of "outside influences." Implicit in this approach is the existence of the "normative Mennonite tradition" and the others that have crept in through the back door. But unlike the "outside influences" school of ecumenicity, this new pluralism school does admit that the Mennonite soul may be nourished by these alternative traditions. The pastoral letter on spirituality, for example, finds all the strands nurturing to the Mennonite search for spirituality.

A differing starting point for the pluralism discussion is James Reimer's "Toward a Christian Theology from a Diversity of Mennonite Perspectives" (1988). He suggests the presence of 13 different theological strands in contemporary Mennonite theologizing:

1. Evolutionary or process theology
2. Shalom theology
3. Liberation theology
4. Narrative theology
5. Feminist theology
6. Anabaptist theology
7. Political theology
8. Historicist theology
9. Existential theology
10. Eschatological theology
11. Evangelical theology
12. Therapeutic theology
13. Ethnic-cultural theology

While Reimer singles out Anabaptist theology as one of the thirteen, he makes it clear that all thirteen forms are current in Mennonite theological reflection. Here is an understanding of pluralism that hints at a different meaning. It is at least partially turned inward and reflexive to examine the heterogeneity that emerges from within our own tradition. This approach not only names the pluralism of the Mennonite world, but by linking the various theological approaches to contemporary Mennonite theology affords the opportunity for open discussion about the many alliances that have been flavored by Anabaptism. Many of these theologies, while having external sources, have also been articulated by people with continuing linkages to "Anabaptism." All have in some fashion emerged from Mennonites theologizing out of their Anabaptist tradition. All can thus enter the dialogue without being assigned stepchild status.

It seems to me that in naming pluralism as the dominant feature of the map, we now need to find a way of naming the many "anabaptisms" that have emerged. Much as our mapping of sixteenth-century Anabaptism has moved from monogenesis to polygenesis, so our mapping of twentieth-century Anabaptism needs to map the polyforms of contemporary Anabaptism. Historically we accept Anabaptist pluralism. Organizationally we accept denominational pluralism. Ideationally have we accepted an Anabaptist pluralism as well as a theological pluralism? Can we name the consequences of the process of interaction between our tradition and modernity and the multiple logics of Anabaptism that now constitute our own self-made pluralism? Do we have a workable taxonomy of the differing kinds of Anabaptisms that now inhabit the pluralist Mennonite world?

NOTES

1 An additional theology not included in either the James Reimer or Norman Kraus map is liturgical theology. I think there is a growing liturgical interest of importance to some Mennonites, particularly those in the diaspora. It is the drift into Episcopal churches and kindred traditions. One New York City Mennonite in categorizing the diaspora population refers to the "sniff and bells crowd." Those Mennonites, feeling a symbolic impoverishment in their own traditions of worship, now find aesthetic meaning in the liturgical forms.

2 I do think we require more than a passing inquiry into national religions. For Americans these have been Republican years. By the accounting of *Mennonite Weekly Review*, we, like the rest of the nation, voted overwhelmingly for Reagan. And Mennonites have not been unaffected by the resurgence of patriotic sentiments. Our ability to yearn after being "a little off center" and the urge to vote Republican is one of the paradoxes that the new map should help to explain.

REFERENCES

Reimer, James
    1988 "Toward a Christian Theology from a Diversity of Men-
        nonite Perspectives." *Conrad Grebel Review* 6:147-159.

FINDING SOCIOLOGICAL ESSENTIALS

CHAPTER 3

SECTARIANISM AND THE SECT CYCLE

Calvin Redekop

An almost unique relationship seems to have developed between the Anabaptist/Mennonite tradition and the sect conceptualization and analysis. The originators of the sociological concept "sect" referred to the Mennonites as the best example of the sect type (Troeltsch, 1960:694; Weber, 1946:306-314). Many subsequent analysts continue to do so (Niebuhr, 1929; Wilson, 1970:8, 17, 32ff.; Yinger, 1957).[1] Beyond this, Mennonites themselves have more-or-less accepted that designation and have spent a great deal of energy trying to understand what sectarianism is and how this helps understand the Mennonite experience and its future. Recent examples include Peter Hamm's *Continuity and Change Among Canadian Mennonite Brethren* and Richard Kyle's *From Sect to Denomination: Church Types and Their Implications for Mennonite Brethren History* (Driedger and Redekop, 1983:36-39; Redekop, 1990).[2]

How can Mennonites as well as others best understand what the Mennonite phenomenon was and continues to be? This question has exercised countless people, and it continues to do so today. What defined Anabaptism's essence in its formative stages, and what is its essential reality today? What utility has the sect typology had in answering this question, and where do people concerned about the future go if the sect interpretation is no longer valid? An answer is needed, since it is becoming increasingly clear that Anabaptism/Mennonitism is confronting a need to recover a clear identity. Some scholars indeed are proposing that the Mennonites are facing an identity crisis (Driedger, 1988; Peachey, 1968; Goertz, 1988; Redekop, 1984). The recent spate of research on identifying the essentials of the Mennonite prospect indicates a ground swell of interest and support in this quest (Driedger, 1973; 1975a; 1977b; 1980a; 1988; Kauffman and Harder, 1975; Hamm, 1987; Harder, 1962, 1971; Redekop and Steiner, 1988).[3]

In order to answer the questions raised above, we need to take a brief excursus into the history of sect theory development and then relate it to the Mennonite experience, and the bases of these factors, come to a conclusion regarding the question of Mennonite identity and whether the sect idea can help us understand where Mennonites are "located" in the schema of things.

A BRIEF HISTORY OF SECTARIAN THEORY

Max Weber and Ernst Troeltsch were two leading early scholars who studied how religious forces affect social forms. Focussing on the Reformation and its aftermath, Weber first developed the sect-church idea and suggested that "A sect is a voluntary association of only those who, according to the principle, are religiously and morally qualified" (Weber, 1946:106). Further, he stated that the church is a "compulsory association for the administration of grace, and the 'sect' is a voluntary association of religiously qualified persons" (Weber, 1946:314). Weber also listed three other characteristics of the sect: the sovereignty of the local sacramental community, strict moral discipline, and a spirit of early Christian brotherhood.

Troeltsch, a colleague of Weber, expanded his typology by refining the church type and then introduced mysticism as a third type. Troeltsch's starting point was that there is a fundamental difference between the way grace comes to humanity. For the church type, "the main question was: How can they gain influence over the masses? Salvation and grace are independent of the measure of subjective realization of strict ethical standards" (Troeltsch, 1960:702). In the course of Christian history there had developed the "great historic powers." These historic powers were the Roman Catholic tradition including its variations (eastern rite, etc.) and the magisterial Reformation churches including the Lutherans and the Reformed. Troeltsch (1960:338) defined the church in contrast to the sect type, and maintained that the church's essence "is its objective institutional character." Its universal character means it will "dominate society, compelling all the members of Society to come under its sphere", for it alone is the "organ of Grace and Redemption" (Troeltsch, 1960:338, 347). But the coercive way in which these powers were used actually helped to plant the seeds of protest by persons who "were entirely opposed to the ecclesiastical system, with its inclusive character and its claim to be the sole depository of grace" (Troeltsch, 1960:702).

One object of this protest was the abolition of domination of one person or set of persons by another. In fact the conflict over the idea of domination was the central issue concerning the differences between the churchly stance and the sectarian protest, as defined by Weber and Troeltsch. A recent elaboration of this stance by Swatos (1979) proposes that the church type of religious organization is identified by the desire to monopolize grace, to be the only institution which dispenses grace and to be able to impose it on everyone in the society, whereas the sect can be classed according to the degrees by which it rejects this stance.

Sect members on the other hand, maintain that religious faith and grace can be mediated only by freedom of belief and that there must be freedom from hierarchy in the way religious sacraments are mediated. The biblical constraints to be humble, submissive, and passive, and even to suffer if need be for the sake of the church, further confirm the presence of the sectarian (Gelassenheit) stance.[4] The separation of sects from Catholicism and Protestantism expresses itself "in an individualistic and subjective method of interpreting the scriptures and in its emphasis upon the attainment of salvation without priesthood or hierarchy" (Troeltsch, 1960:702).

According to Troeltsch (1960:703) the central characteristic of the sect type is that the sectarians work from the bottom up (from the position of the common person or common humanity) while the church works from the top down. The lay ministry, the locus of authority in the congregation, the refusal to participate in the state which exercises power over others, the simple lifestyle, the mutual-aid practices, the strict rules regarding ethical practices, the expulsion of deviants--these and many other practices are understood in the idea of the sect, that is, the refusal to assume the monopoly of grace. This refusal of a hierarchy to dominate or control religious life is a very helpful concept in explaining Anabaptist-Mennonite social structure both in terms of understanding their origins as well as understanding the relevance of this idea for their existence today.

This description of the conditions during the Reformation and subsequent years proved to be a powerful and creative analysis. It is with good reason that the Weber-Troeltsch typology has become a classic analysis, one which still is useful today if its limitations are understood. The first limitation is the obvious one (but almost always ignored), that the conceptualization was derived from a specific European context, and was not meant to become a universally applicable concept. It is important to note that Weber never assumed that the sect type would persist indefinitely. He assumed that it would succumb to the process of secularization.

Through his experience in America, Weber (1946:306-11) observed that "otherworldly sects" became middle class through the emergence of voluntary organizations which became substitutes for the exclusive brotherhood.

Further, Troeltsch as a sequel to his magnum opus, *The Social Teachings of the Christian Churches*, wrote *Protestantism and Progress*, in which he indicated what Protestantism contributed to the development of the modern spirit. In reference to the sects Troeltsch (1958:123-25) says, "It was now at last the turn of the stepchildren of the Reformation to have their great hour in the history of the world," to implement their "influence on the world" including separation, toleration, voluntarism, liberty, and inviolability of the inner life. And it is precisely the role of freedom of belief which was the mortar of the great changes in religious structure, especially in North America, which Troeltsch indicated had changed the nature of contemporary religion.

Hence, Weber and Troeltsch assumed that church and sect were historically conditioned events that would evolve in time, and that because conditions would never be the same again so the typology would not be usable as such (Redekop, 1962). Another obvious limitation of the original conceptualization was that the sect, which by definition stood in opposition to the dominating church and profane society, and emerged in separation from it, would by that very fact become transformed in the subsequent dialectical relationships with the opposing forces. Hence, regardless of the original intentions of the sect group, it would be forced to change, as an analysis of most sect groups shows (Redekop, 1974).

Another limitation which has rarely been discussed is the fact that the dominant church type has itself disappeared in North America as well as been modified in Europe, so that the religious protest dimension has lost its importance. For example, under the pluralistic norms operative in North America there are no dominant religious institutions which can coerce any individual or group to conform to its dogma or its practices. Further, the profane society has also changed dramatically so that the coercion which occurred during the Reformation is no longer as severe. For example, the state in North America no longer assists the church in collecting tithes for the support of the clergy. This is especially important when we discuss the concept of the denomination later.

These limitations were not immediately clear to social scientists, and a spate of research and theorizing regarding the sectarian nature of religious movements emerged. Numerous studies resulted which attempted to establish classification schemes so that the variety of religious groups could be subsumed and studied.

Included in this development were scholars such as Elmer Clark (1949) who developed five classes of sects--Pessimistic or Adventist, Perfectionist or Subjectivist, Charismatic or Pentecostal, Communistic, and Legalistic or Objectivistic. Later Wilson (1970) developed another system which included conversionist, revolutionist, introversionist, manipulationist, thaumaturgical, reformist, and utopian. Others including Yinger (1957) who developed the sixfold typology of cult, sect, established sect, class church/denomination, ecclesia and universal church introduced a "flood of types based upon a variety of criteria" which seemed to become totally incomprehensible (Swatos, 1979:5ff).

But regardless of the definitions developed, one of the most interesting and provocative ancillary insights concerned the accommodation of the sect to the secular society, the so called "sect cycle theory." H. Richard Niebuhr (1929) having understood Weber and Troeltsch, first "observed that the sect, if defined rigorously in the terms presented here, cannot last beyond the founding generation" (O'Dea, 1968:131). Niebuhr (1929) clearly delineated the "sequential pattern in the course of which sects themselves are accommodated to the secular society and make their own compromise with the world" (O'Dea, 1968:131). Liston Pope (1942) is best known for his careful description of the secularization process in his *Millhands and Preachers* in which he describes how the variety of sect groups in the Gaston community became "church like." A host of other research followed including O'Dea's research on the secularization of the Mormons, Val Clear's (1958) research on the Church of God, Donald Royer's (1955) study of the Church of the Brethren, and others. The conclusion to the majority of these studies was that most groups underwent a definite change from a puristic and ascetic rejection of profane society to an accommodating and accepting stance toward the world (Redekop, 1959).[5]

These studies showed that there was change, secularization, accommodation, and the like. Yinger (1957) subsumed much of the research results in his famous six-fold typology which included the "sect" and "established sect," by which a vast variety of religious groups, not considered "mainline churches," were analyzed and classified. Subsequently, Swatos (1979:11) has developed a further elaboration into "sect, entrenched sect, dynamic sect, and established sect". But the ability to generalize from these conceptualizations has been weak or non-existent. What did the fact that the Church of the Brethren changed and became an established sect (for example) contribute to the general knowledge of social forces? Change is as natural as stability. This fact has been the stumbling block, and it has forced social scientists to recognize that every religious group has unique historical antecedents, and must be understood in its historical context and development (Redekop, 1975). Hence, the sect phenomenon is useful if the definition is agreed upon and accepted, and the specific experience of the particular sect group is adequately known.

For the purposes of this analysis, we will continue to use the definition that Troeltsch provided, which as we indicated is focused basically on the Anabaptist/Mennonite tradition, namely: 1) a church consisting only of believers; 2) voluntary membership; 3) church discipline including excommunication; 4) rejection of the efficacy of sacraments; 5) emphasis on holy life including rejection of the state role in church, rejection of oaths, refusal of violence, taking up the cross; 6) equality and mutuality; and 7) following the Sermon on the Mount (Troeltsch, 1958:694-705; Redekop, 1959; 1962; 1965; 1975; 1989). The sociological consequences of this typology is a drastic separation from the rest of society, religious and secular, and this therefore forms the basis for a dualistic theology and practice (i.e. separation from the world) in Mennonite life and thought.

In the general application of sect/church typology, therefore, there are a number of factors which are of central importance: 1) the historical conditions operating in the emergence of the "sect"; 2) the nature of the opposition and support the group has experienced by the surrounding society; 3) the nature of the internal "dilemmas," contradictions or ideologies which will affect the life and development of the sect; and 4) the degree to which societal conditions have changed in the direction of the sectarian protest.

MENNONITE SECTARIANISM: A PREDICTABLE CYCLE?

The Troeltschian church-sect cycle which he developed around the turn of the century, has considerable power in helping to explain the origin of the Anabaptist-Mennonite movement; indeed it still offers considerable insight to the process of defining and analyzing Mennonite life, and it has been used more than any other perspective (Driedger and Redekop, 1983). At the same time it must be noted that most Mennonites including the most conservative would in daily practice deny the designation "sect" because of its derogatory connotation.

But the sect conceptualization must be of some use in Mennonite self understanding, if we want to continue to use it. Obviously the question of how Anabaptism/Mennonitism has fared in the light of its original goals and life will show whether the sectarian conceptualization may be helpful, or whether the concept needs to be expanded or changed, or forsaken entirely. To this we now turn.

There is no question that the concern about the loss of original "sectarian" purity has been a fact for many Mennonites. One celebrated schism (among many) which expressed very well the reluctance to relinquish the sectarian stance was the Holdeman schism of Ohio in the mid-1850s. John Holdeman had begun to realize that "the church had strayed from the 'right and true ground' and had accepted many unconverted members. The decay of the church troubled him and he admonished the members for worldly and flippant conversations" (Hiebert 1973:176). The acrimonious debate which developed contributed to the formation of a group which wanted to return to the basics as Menno Simons and others had commanded. "When a church lapses so far from the Word of God that one becomes a transgressor by remaining in it, because the members refuse to reform, one can only be obedient by going out," Holdeman said (Hiebert, 1973:183).

From their beginnings Mennonites have been concerned about the maintenance of their original commitment, especially as expressed in their relationship to the world. The idea of the two kingdoms, the one holy and coming from God, the other apostate and degenerate, resulted in a stance of nonconformity to the world, and rejection of linking with the state and religious institutions. This dominated Mennonite thinking for four centuries. "The New Testament vision of the church in the world is characterized by a singular duality. Behind this duality lies the concept of the two kingdoms. The one is 'the dominion of darkness,' the kingdom of this world; the other is 'the kingdom of his beloved Son'" (Bender, 1962:112). The central theological and normative thrust has been how the "colony of Heaven" or "the people of God" has been expressed in history and whether it has been faithful to God's call. Hence the ongoing debate in the Mennonite community has been, "What does it mean to be faithful members of God's kingdom?" (Redekop, 1990).

The inevitable involvement of cultural forms in this search has produced the uneasy process of trying to determine which cultural forms are faithful and which are not, and hence Paul Peachey (1957:334) suggests that one of the basic dilemmas for Mennonites has been to understand culture and their relationship to it. It was in this context that H. Richard Niebuhr proposed that the Mennonite society was a form of "Christ against culture." This was however a thorough misunderstanding of Mennonite faith, because Mennonites never rejected culture as such, only those expressions which they thought would hinder the realization of the Kingdom of God. Mennonites have simply always subordinated specific cultural forms to the primacy of community life (Redekop, 1976).

A number of major understandings have emerged which

attempt to understand what has indeed taken place in the Mennonite tradition to provide an answer to the above question. One understanding, which has not had much credence, is to maintain that the Mennonites have moved from sect to "established sect," which according to Yinger, is a situation in which the Mennonite movement has become an institutionalized sectarian group. Although there is little literature that promotes this view (Harder, 1962; Kyle, 1985), it has utility for describing the conservative Old Order groups which continue to maintain their traditional protest and separation stance. Most theorists believe that these groups have not remained merely as they were originally, but have accrued ethnic characteristics (Redekop and Hostetler, 1977). This however does not obviate the theory proposed by Yinger and Swatos that sect groups can stagnate and remain relatively stable for a considerable period of time. Swatos proposes that the Anglican church in fact evidenced "established sect" characteristics in North America.

The entrenched sect or established sect theory has not received much attention in reference to Mennonites because of a much more prevalent idea, namely the idea that the Mennonites have historically moved from a sect type (as defined for the Mennonites by Troeltsch) to an ethnic group. This was first introduced by E. K. Francis, (1948, 1955) an astute student of Mennonites. Though he does not deny the religious foundations, he proposes that economic successes "were bought at the price of institutionalization of religion and secularization of the inner life of the group" (Francis, 1955:27). Many other Mennonite historians and sociologists have followed this interpretation, including Driedger, Kraybill, P. Toews, and Redekop.

This has become such an accepted interpretation that a major debate has emerged (see Redekop and Steiner), and has resulted in a polemical debate, illustrated best by the argument presented by John Redekop in *A People Apart*, which assumes that Mennonites are basically identified by their ethnic traits and need to reject these traits if Anabaptism is to survive. This argument has been strongly rejected by Calvin Redekop (1948) whose article "Anabaptism and the ethnic Ghost," argues that Anabaptism by definition demands a separated life which expresses itself in specific cultural forms, but that these forms are attempts at becoming a people of God, which by definition will appear to be sub-cultural forms. Thus what can be seen as pure traditionalizing of a religious faith is actually much more complex, and must be seen as the attempt to express culturally the precepts of the mandates of becoming a people of God.[6]

Another major interpretation of Mennonite movement from the pure sectarian position is the movement from sect to denomination, a major theoretical stance of many sociologists; this has also been accepted by Mennonite sociologists and historians (Kauffman and Harder, 1975; Kaufman, 1931; Sawatsky, 1983). There are several responses to this issue. First, from a theoretical perspective as was argued above the idea of the denomination must be restricted to the North American context, so that groups that emerged in Europe have a different origin and cannot be fit into that scheme without considerable ingenuity (Friedmann, 1956:37-38). So from that perspective, to say that Mennonites have become a denomination demands drastic accommodation, which is difficult.

But the more powerful fact which precludes describing the Mennonites as having denominationalized is the fact that the denomination has been most adequately defined as that religious group that accepts pluralism as normative (each religious group should be considered as valid as another) and at the same time accepts the dominant culture/society as legitimate (Swatos, 1979). This latter factor has introduced into North American Christianity an acceptance of a new form of "denomination", namely, the dictates of mass culture and values--civil religion, if you will.

Denominationalism is an American response to the diversity of religious expression and to the dominant culture (Mead, 1977; Richey, 1977; Smith, 1977). Thus it is rather naive to define the Mennonites as a denomination (or as a group of denominations!) unless one wants to suggest that Mennonites have changed their belief in the validity of their original protest, or have totally lost their separateness and believe that North America is the promised land. Though there has been considerable "apostasy" in the eyes of some, few Mennonites would suggest that, according to the definition presented here, Mennonites have become denominations.

Nevertheless numerous scholars have argued that Mennonites have become more like denominations because of secularization, or by accommodating to the secular society, as Friedmann does in the article cited above. Karl Baehr (1942), Peter Hamm (1987), Leland Harder (1962), Kauffman and Harder (1975), Kaufman (1931), Franklin Littel (1962), and S. F. Pannabecker (1977), to list some of the major scholars, have proposed that the Mennonite church has been involved in becoming denominational. By this they apparently mean that a considerable degree of secularization or accommodation to the prevailing secular order has taken place. One of the most interesting is Edmund G. Kaufman's (1931:46) theory that the North American Mennonites relinquished their sectarian position as they adopted the prevailing values: "Gradually the customs, practices, ideals, and doctrines of the two groups (the society and the Mennonites) more or less conform and the sect is again slowly fused with the larger community by ceasing to exist, or becoming a denomination gradually federating with similar bodies." In the same vein, Kauffman and Harder (1975:297) say that they "examined the distinctive patterns of development and adaptation to the North American environment. In that connection [Chapter 2] the concept of 'secularization' was mentioned as supplying one interpretation of these denominational patterns in relation to each other." Consequently, the authors' comparisons of the Mennonites to the predominant denominations have been rather strongly criticized because it amounts to comparing apples and oranges.

Since it is so widely used, secularization is a most confusing term with many meanings. In the present volume Hamm deals with the concept, and thus the definition we will use is based on the elements he discusses. Though I would not fully agree with Hamm's interpretation, in general I accept it. Secularization here is restricted to the point of view of the religious groups, namely, the Mennonites, and hence is focused more on the increasing conformity with this world. Shiner's points 2, 3 and 5 (Hamm, *infra*) might compose a satisfactory set of components. So we define secularization as the acceptance of the values of mass culture and a modern positivistic world view. This could be the key variable in the denominationalization of Mennonites, but then this would be tantamount to accepting generally accepted definitions of Christian and non-Christian values and behavior as they apply to North American society as normative, and comparing Mennonites and other religious groups on this scale, a practice which will strike most Mennonites as odd. To this must be added the problem with the definition of secularization, which at present is in a great state of confusion and disagreement (Ainlay, *infra*, etc.) Nevertheless, if acceptance of major North American values and practices is taken as a criterion of denominationalization, then Mennonites are becoming denominations. But this is assuming that denominationalism is a matter of assimilation. This however does violence to a responsible use of terms and concepts which has been proposed by scholars noted above.

Another approach to the sect-cycle theory is the structural disequilibrium analysis, which has been applied to Mennonites by Leland Harder (1962). This theory suggests that social groups often contain values or goals which are inherently contradictory. As applied to Mennonites, Harder proposes that the Mennonite sectarian goal of separation and retention of purity has been contradicted by the equally powerful goal of evangelism and outreach. Thus, as the Mennonite conferences tried to retain their faithfulness to the "Sermon on the Mount" ethic, they found this implied outreach and sharing with the unregenerate world, which created an unworkable tension. "It is precisely those sects which show most

concern for maintenance of the two decisive criteria for their existence in the most pristine form--voluntarism and separatism--that
wrestle most with the problem of disequilibrium" (1962:31). Disequilibrium in Harder's analysis expressed itself in conflict and
schism on the one hand, and adopting the fundamentalist and
evangelical approaches on the other. Thus, insofar as Mennonites
have adopted these theological orientations, which are symptomatic
of most Protestant sect-type groups in North America, this can be
seen as a sign of denominationalization (Harder, 1962).

The concept of structural disequilibrium is a useful concept,
and in one sense one of several major factors in understanding the
dynamics of Mennonite change. That is, it is clear that internal
forces and contradictions cause a group to change; on the other
hand, the encounter with the environment cannot be ignored, and it
is just as influential in determining the nature of the sectarian
group's change to something else. Hence both internal and external
factors and variables have been instrumental in the evolution of the
Mennonite project. What is needed is some sort of bench mark to
analyze how the Mennonite society has changed, and what the
dynamics of this change have been. Although each person may have
his/her own method or paradigm, the next section will present my
own attempt to understand where the Mennonite movement has
come from, and where it is going.

THE MENNONITE MOVEMENT AND THE ORIGINAL SEC-
TARIAN VISION

In the last chapter of *The Recovery of the Anabaptist Vision*,
Paul Peachey (1957:335) raised the crucial question for Mennonite
thought and life when he asked, "Does the Anabaptist vision still call
today toward a different kind of Christian living, as it did four
centuries ago?" The answer to this question will determine how we
will evaluate the sect cycle dynamic, or how we will need to change
it. If we assume that Anabaptism is still in some fashion in keeping
with its original prophetic vision, then we will answer the question
differently than if we assume it has drastically changed.

The position, which I have recently outlined in several places
(Redekop, 1988; 1989) is that Anabaptism/Mennonitism was and is
basically a utopian movement, and that its very raison-d'-être has
been to attempt to keep this vision alive. This is the position
Rosemary Ruether (1970) also takes, among others. In this context,
I define utopian as that which was defined as unrealizable by the
established authorities (Redekop, 1989), but which simply meant a
restoration of the pure ideal of the New Testament church. The

Anabaptists fully expected that the church could be renewed and restored, if only people, especially those in authority, would take the biblical teachings seriously (Ruether, 1970). The ideals for which the Anabaptists strove are precisely those which were outlined above by Max Weber and Ernst Troeltsch. The pure church, obtained by separating from the corrupt church and pagan society, was the utopian goal.

Although theological and philosophical elements could be used as the basis for the subsequent analysis, I choose to focus on the more sociological variables, especially since it is generally assumed that Mennonites are basically an attempt to actualize the ethical call of the Christian gospel. We look at several central factors.

Accommodating to Mass Culture

As was alluded to above, much of the sectarian analysis has had to do with cultural separation. Mennonite acceptance or rejection of cultural factors is a misunderstanding of the Mennonite goal, since cultural elements as such were never the issue. The issue was, "How does a specific cultural element affect our life in the kingdom of God?" Thus in this context, the index of Anabaptist authenticity is to ask in what way has cultural assimilation affected the "peoplehood" and prophetic witness? In this view then, the question is, "In contrast with the early Anabaptist lifestyle, has the adoption of specific modern cultural artifacts such as education affected the authenticity of recent Mennonites?"

The answer to this question is very difficult to obtain, and there are varying views. The Old Order Mennonite groups, including Holdeman Mennonites, continue to believe that modernity is inimical to true community and Christian faith (Hostetler, 1969; Hiebert, 1973; Kraybill, 1989; Redekop, 1969). The recent study of the Old Order Amish by Kraybill provides new insight into the process of understanding how culture affects faith. Most modern Mennonites have come to the conclusion that technology is totally neutral and that it does not have any implications for religion, but this itself indicates the degree of cultural capitulation. Wiser heads among us are saying convincingly that technology (one aspect of culture) is not neutral, that is has profound affects on how we live and relate (Ellul, 1964; Grant, 1969). My conclusion is that Mennonites have become more influenced by modern mass culture, especially in its technological form, than is normally recognized, and that modernity is a basic assumption of Mennonites (Kraybill, in Redekop and Steiner).[7] The quality of human relationships in the Mennonite society, both in the congregational and in the social context, has become increasingly individualistic. Kauffman and Harder (1975:323) state that "communalism ranks tenth for power to predict dependent variables." Without presenting more evidence because of space considerations, the "sectarian" trait of "brotherhood" as Troeltsch defined it, is suffering as a result of cultural adaptations. This topic impinges on the modernization issue, and to some degree secularization. Secularization was discussed earlier, but modernization needs elaboration. Kraybill's chapter in this present volume addresses this subject, and I accept his general definition as acceptable: "modernization not only revamps the social organization or social architecture of an entire society; it also penetrates our collective consciousness and alters our ways of thinking." The latter element is especially important since it focuses on the particular religious group.

Mutuality

The principle of mutuality, expressed in egalitarianism, lay leadership, mutual sharing and assistance, and many other expressions, have been proposed as a central element of Anabaptism (Weber/Troeltsch, *et. al.*). There is little need to specify the great historical expression of mutuality in congregational and community life. In the contemporary context, this mutuality has become rather formally institutionalized, such as for example in the Mennonite Mutual Aid Association, not to mention others such as the mutual insurance organizations, etc. The loss of this dimension is rather difficult to analyze and measure since the mutual aid equivalents of today are different than they were several hundred years ago. The egalitarianism of economic life, so central to early Anabaptism, has clearly changed, and some of the more tragic epochs of Mennonite history pertain to economic disparities and inequities such as evidenced in the Russian Mennonite commonwealth.

The disparities in economic wealth and income, to say nothing of consumption patterns among Mennonites, are increasing, as most knowledgeable people will admit. The Old Orders are still able to restrict these disparities, but the pressures are increasing there as well. The Kauffman and Harder (1975:62) study indicates that there were almost 20% in the over $15,000 income bracket, while there were 21.8% in the under $3,000 bracket. It does not increase the impact to know that Mennonites in general are a bit above the national average in income. The seduction of materialism and economic power are clearly gnawing at the vital organs of lay congregationalism and brotherhood, as Troeltsch indicated.

Individualism is another way of discussing secularization and modernization. It affects mutuality directly. Mennonites have always been concerned about the centrality of the "love of the sister and brother." Individualism is exactly the opposite (see Ainlay). Ainlay asks the critical question for this point, "Have the biblical and civic traditions of Mennonite culture been weakened or replaced by utilitarian and expressive individualism?" He answers the question this way: "There have been some changes in Mennonite life, which we can already document, that might give us reason to believe that this shift might be occurring."

Adult Baptism and Voluntarism

Several of Troeltsch's concepts regarding the sect type can be subsumed under the concept of adult baptism and voluntarism in church life. There is some evidence that these principles and practices have eroded. Certainly the age of baptism provides some evidence, and it has been moving more and more into the younger years, indicating an accommodation to prevailing North American practices. The median age of baptism for Mennonites of all persuasions is 14.9 years, prompting Melvin Gingerich to ask, "What does this mean in the context of our historic understanding of the responsible decision demanded of those who accept the Christian life" (Kauffman and Harder, 1975:71). Even though the Mennonites generally scored higher on voluntarism and baptism than American denominations such as the Presbyterians, the differences are not impressive.

The Ethical Life

Troeltsch stressed the importance of the Sermon on the Mount as a cardinal point of the sect. It is now generally believed that Anabaptism was based less on abstract visions of how the new society ought to look than on a vision which demanded that the Christian disciple bring his life into alignment with the Christian confession that had already been made (Burkholder, 1959).

This factor may be one of the most sensitive barometers of Anabaptist life, and at the same time the most difficult to determine or understand. Again Kauffman and Harder (1975:129) conclude that "the followers of Anabaptists still exercise a rigorous discipline in matters of personal morality." Personal morality has been central to Anabaptism, but social morality has been equally important and it is here that some slippage is observed. Kauffman and Harder (1975:149) state that there is a tug and pull in two directions, one toward normative Anabaptism, the other toward the secular societal practices. The position of Mennonites on race equality, peace issues including serving in the military, and social concerns about poverty and inequality, is increasingly mixed and uneven, indicating that Mennonites are no longer unified on what the "Sermon on the Mount" is actually teaching.

Congregation, Family and Community

The sectarian definition of Troeltsch and many others has always stressed the importance of the congregation, family, and community in providing discipline, leadership, and care for members. In fact in the earlier period of Anabaptism, these three facets were actually one. In the Hutterite and Old Order groups, it is still rather that way. The mutual dependency and support of each of these elements for the other is illustrated by most Old Order Amish communities or by the Mennonites in the Chaco of Paraguay. In the North American context, these three are not nearly as supportive of each other, and in fact, the community is largely absent.

This is a complex issue, and it is difficult to show how the family, congregation and community are being split or are being weakened, and how the changes are affecting each other. Certainly the breakdown of Mennonite families is increasing, and it is logical to suppose that the influences of the Mennonite community and congregation are lessening and the values of the secular society are becoming more insistent (Yoder, 1983; Redekop, 1989).

These five elements may be a useful way to translate the original sectarian conceptualization into contemporary language so we can relate it to the factors we are now able to observe today. The Mennonite sectarian stance is different then it was originally, but conditions have changed, as has the internal self understanding of the Mennonites themselves. Thus for example, the basic concept of freedom of religious faith and commitment, which the Anabaptists helped to create, is now an accepted value and is at the basis of the pluralistic denominational structure of North America, as indicated above. What can be said that will help to understand "where the Mennonites have been, and where they are going?"

SUMMARY

The sect typology has been profitably used to understand Mennonite origins, dynamics and prospects. In the preceding discussion, we have attempted to conceptualize the Mennonite entity using the sectarian mold. Is there progress in our understanding of Anabaptist/Mennonitism so that the sect typology needs to be superseded?

Or is the best road to understanding still the Troeltschian model? As indicated in section one, I believe that it has little value if it is used in its generally evolved sociological sense. If however we accept the concept as Troeltsch originally attempted, to describe the specifics of the Reformation struggle, then there are still some aspects which are relevant, and I have tried to focus on some of them. The questions whether Mennonites are a sect or church, an "established sect" or denomination something else, however, are rather questionable, since these questions mix the original valid concept with later elaborations attempting to generalize a specific historical period, which confused the issues and made the concept less useful. To know that the Mennonites are a denomination is not helpful since it provides us with no basis for comparison or judgment in regard to its own vision and purposes; but to know that it has lost its voluntary nature is very helpful, if we agree that voluntarism was a central aspect of its original nature, and if we know whether that principle has suffered.

All sociological concepts and measures are created to be functional--that is, they should be helpful in understanding our social and cultural existence. The sect type has done that, but it has also confused us. The reality for us was the fact that during the Reformation, individuals, families, and groups mobilized to protest the corruption and decay of society and religion, and set out to change society (at least themselves and their families) to approximate more the ideal commanded in Scripture and by the life and admonitions of Jesus. It is important to know what those issues were, what significance they had then, and whether they have any significance now. The sect type has lifted out some of those significant issues, but the theological and historical disciplines as well as the rank and file membership can be just as helpful in sorting these factors.

Hence the concern about acculturation, assimilation, decay, secularization, materialism, splintering, and loss of fervor and spirituality, points to a more important question than understanding whether the Mennonites are still a sect. The ultimate question is: Has the fire gone out? Is the Mennonite similar to the church at Sardis of whom John said, "I know thy works, that thou hast a name that thou livest, and art dead" (Rev. 3:1). Fortunately only God knows the answer and is in a position to answer this question. But this should not keep us from asking the question, for it is desperately important to know whether we are dead but still think we are alive. I personally believe that conceptualizing the Mennonite vision as a utopian movement which set out to incarnate the beliefs and practices of New Testament Christianity totally into contemporary reality is an easier and more convincing way to look at this phenomenon (Redekop and Steiner, 1988). A utopian vision is a more open and responsive stance than a sectarian one, at least as it has been understood by the established powers such as the church, the state, and social scientists who are attempting to create a universally applicable concept, which does not do justice to the Spirit of God.

A utopian vision allows for the larger society to change, for that indeed is the utopian's purpose. Further, it is my conviction that the Anabaptist utopian movement itself has changed. First, it's agenda is different, for many of the issues for which early members bled and died have been adopted; e.g., today people are relatively free to choose to believe or to remain apostate. Christians are free, in Western countries at least, to refrain from killing and using violence. Christians are free to form voluntary congregations of believers and to engage in strong congregational discipline including excommunication. Christians are now free to practice unlimited mutual assistance and practice high ethical standards, both in the community and without. The "pagan" world has changed considerably.

Further, the persecuting religious structure has changed, so that the relationship of the rest of Christendom is vastly different. Anabaptists no longer need to fear the church. In fact Anabaptist/Mennonites are now being invited to sit down at banquets celebrating fraternity and common purposes with other Christian groups. The Mennonites are now "in the world," but the world has changed. Are they more "of the world than the early forefathers and mothers?" I believe the utopian vision is a better paradigm for the contemporary analysis than the sectarian because it allows us to ask, "What are the relevant and signally important commitments to which God is calling us today?" We can involve ourselves in that question and try to contribute to its answer.

NOTES

1 The research and bibliography on sectarianism is huge. The article in the *International Encyclopedia of the Social Sciences* is basic, and provides some bibliography. An annotated bibliography of sect and cult research is provided by Ira E. Harrison, *A Selected, Annotated Bibliography on Store-Front Churches and other Religious Writings*, which is very helpful, though unfortunately ends in 1962; *Social Scientific Studies of Religion: A Bibliography* produced by Berkowitz and Johnson presents an extensive listing until 1967. The booklet by Swatos, *Into Denominationalism*, provides a good recent bibliography. The *Journal of the Scientific Study of Religion* published an index which includes sectarian articles and books published until 1981. Little new material has appeared since then that offers any appreciable shift in conceptualization. My own attempt to come to terms with the concept is contained in an unpublished manuscript entitled "The Sect Idea" (1976).

2 The use of the sect conceptualization by Mennonite scholars to analyze Mennonites has been almost total. See Driedger and Redekop, 1983; also Redekop, 1959).

3 The Mennonite identity question has been exercising Mennonites for many decades, but it is coming into great prominence in recent years. For the most comprehensive analysis of the issue, and related bibliography, see *Mennonite Identity: Historical and Contemporary Perspectives* by Redekop and Steiner (1988). For many people, the increasing salience of this question is prima facie evidence that the Mennonite "sect" has dissolved.

4 It is interesting that the idea originally promoted by Troeltsch that Anabaptist sectarians reflect the common person, that they represent the position of weakness and submissiveness, and that they are identified with the weak and the poor has not found conscious linkage with the theological and historical emphasis on "Gelassenheit", humility and passivity of Mennonites. It has been long assumed that the Mennonite tradition expressed Gelassenheit, but that it has a more than incidental connection to their very existence as a group has not been widely discussed. See Joe Liechty, "Humility: The Foundation of Mennonite Religious Outlook in the 1860's" (1980).

5 The application of the sect cycle model to religious groups has been remarkably wide. For partial bibliography, see my *The Sectarian Black and White World*. The bibliography by Swatos presents additional studies, as does the Berkowitz and Johnson book. Groups which have been studied with this framework in mind include the Baptists, Church of the Brethren, the Church of God, Holiness groups, Jehovah's Witnesses, Mormons, Mennonites, Methodists, Pentecostals, Seventh Day Adventists, and Quakers, to name just a few. Many of these focused on the economic transformation of the sect, by which the sect moved to the "churchly" position as it achieved economic status. This derived from the "economic disinheritance" theory which Niebuhr (1929) included in his "sect-cycle" theory.

6 David Martin has caught the essentials of this problem when he states, "From some viewpoints the sect is even further removed from the denomination than it is from the church. The elements of pragmatism and continuous social adjustment found in the denomination are entirely foreign to sectarianism.... The denomination is aware of independent orders of truth and of alternative aspects of truth. But the sect recognizes no alternative or independent orders of truth outside the inclusiveness of its own vision" (Martin, 1966:184).

7 The Mennonite understanding of the "world" and "worldliness" has not been carefully analyzed. A full theology of creation and of the world has not yet emerged, but it is clear that Anabaptists did not reject the creation or the world but rather worldly or "pagan" society. Again David Martin (1966:183) states the issue clearly: "Amongst the sects about to be discussed the Society of Friends provides the clearest example of a Christian sectarianism which, although it rejects society, is nevertheless 'at one' with creation." I have stated elsewhere (1986) that Mennonites have never been opposed to culture, only those forms which inhibited the full fruition of the Christian message. By mass culture, therefore, I refer to those values, practices, and technologies which militate against the goals of the Kingdom of heaven.

REFERENCES

Baehr, Karl
 1942 "Secularization among the Mennonites of Elkhart County,
  Indiana." *Mennonite Quarterly Review* 16:131-160.

Bender, H. S.
 1962 *These Are My People*. Scottdale: Herald Press.

Burkholder, J. Lawrence
 1959 "Ethics." *Mennonite Encyclopedia* 4:1079-1083.

Clark, Elmer T.
 1949 *The Small Sects in America*. Nashville: Abingdon-
  Cokesbury Press. 1949.

Clear, Val
 1958 "The Church of God: A Study in Social Adaptation."
  Unpublished Ph.D. dissertation, University of Chicago.

Driedger, Leo
 1975 "Canadian Mennonite Urbanism: Ethnic Villagers or
  Metropolitan Remnant?" *Mennonite Quarterly Review*
  49:226-241.

Driedger, Leo
 1977 "The Anabaptist Identification Ladder: Plain-Urbane
  Continuity in Diversity." *Mennonite Quarterly Review*
  51:278-291.

Driedger, Leo
 1988 *Mennonite Identity in Conflict*. Lewiston: The Edwin
  Mellon Press.

Driedger, Leo and Jacob Peters
 1976 "Ethnic Identity: A Comparison of Mennonites and
  Other German Students." *Mennonite Quarterly Review*
  47:225-244.

Driedger, Leo and Calvin Redekop
 1983 "Sociology of the Mennonites: State of the Arts and
  Science." *Journal of Mennonite Studies* 1:33-63.

Ellul, Jacques
    1964 *The Technological Society.* New York: Vintage Books.

Fretz, J. Winfield, and Harold S. Bender
    1957 "Mutual Aid." *Mennonite Encyclopedia* 3. Scottdale: Herald Press.

Francis, Emerick K.
    1948 "The Russian Mennonites: from Religious to Ethnic Group." *American Journal of Sociology* 54:101-107.

Francis, Emerick K.
    1955 *In Search of Utopia: The Mennonites in Manitoba.* Glencoe, IL: Free Press.

Friedmann, Robert
    1956 "Denomination." *Mennonite Encyclopedia* 2:37-38.

Grant, George
    1969 *Technology and Empire.* Toronto: House of Anansi.

Hamm, Peter
    1987 *Continuity and Change Among Canadian Mennonite Brethren.* Waterloo: Wilfrid Laurier Press.

Harder, Leland
    1962 "The Quest for Equilibrium in an Established Sect: A Study of Social Change in the General Conference Church." Unpublished Ph.D. dissertation, Northwestern University.

Harder, Leland
    1971 "An Empirical Search for the Key Variable in Mennonite Reality." *Mennonite Quarterly Review* 45:331-351.

Hershberger, Guy F.
    1957 "The Recovery of the Anabaptist Vision." Scottdale: Herald Press.

Hershberger, Guy F.
    1958 "The Way of the Cross in Human Relations." Scottdale: Herald Press.

Hiebert, Clarence
    1973 *The Holdeman People.* S. Pasadena, CA: William Carey
        Library.

Hostetler, John A.
    1954 *The Sociology of Mennonite Evangelism.* Scottdale:
        Herald Press.

Johnson, Benton
    1957 "A Critical Appraisal of the Church-Sect Typology."
        American Sociological Review, 22:88-92.

Kauffman, J. Howard and Leland Harder
    1975 *Anabaptists Four Centuries Later.* Scottdale: Herald
        Press.

Kaufman, Edmund G.
    1931 *The Development of the Missionary and Philanthropic
        Interest among the Mennonites of North America.* Berne,
        IN: Mennonite Book Concern.

Kraybill, Don
    1988 "Modernity and Identity: The Transformation of Men-
        nonite Ethnicity." In Calvin Redekop and Samuel
        Steiner (Eds.), *Mennonite Identity: Historical and Con-
        temporary Perspectives.* New York: University Press of
        America.

Kraybill, Don
    1989 *The Riddle of Amish Culture.* Baltimore: Johns Hopkins
        Press.

Kyle, Richard G.
    1985 *From Sect to Denomination: Church Types and their
        Implications for Mennonite Brethren Today.* Hillsboro:
        Center for Mennonite Brethren Studies.

Littell, Franklin
    1962 *From State Church to Pluralism.* New York: Dou-
        bleday/Anchor.

Martin, David
    1966 *Pacifism: An Historical and Sociological Study.* New
        York: Schocken Books.

Mead, Sidney
    1977 "Denominationalism: The Shape of Protestantism in America." In Russel Richey (Ed.), *Denominationalism*. Nashville: Abingdon.

O'Dea, Thomas
    1968 "Sects and Cults." *International Encyclopedia of the Social Sciences*, 130-136.

Pannabecker, S. F.
    1977 *Open Doors: The History of the General Conference Mennonite Church*. Newton: Faith and Life Press.

Peachey, Paul
    1957 "The Recovery of the Anabaptist Vision." In Guy F. Hershberger (Ed.), *The Recovery of the Anabaptist Vision*. Scottdale: Herald Press.

Peachy, Paul
    1968 "Identity Crisis among American Mennonites." *Mennonite Quarterly Review* 42:243-259.

Pope, Liston
    1942 *Millhands and Preachers*. New Haven: Yale University Press.

Redekop, Calvin
    1959 "The Sectarian Black and White World." Unpublished Ph.D. Dissertation, University of Chicago.

Redekop, Calvin
    1990 "Sectarianism and Cultural Mandate." *Mennonite Encyclopedia*, 5. Scottdale: Herald Press.

Redekop, Calvin
    1962 "The Sect Cycle in Perspective." *Mennonite Quarterly Review* 36:155-161.

Redekop, Calvin
    1965 "The Sect Cycle from a New Perspective." *Mennonite Quarterly Review* 39:204-213.

Redekop, Calvin
    1969 *The Old Colony Mennonites: Dilemmas of Ethnic Minor-
          ity Life*. Baltimore: Johns Hopkins Press.

Redekop, Calvin
    1974   "Anabaptism and the Ethnic Ghost." *Mennonite
           Quarterly Review* 53:133-46.

Redekop, Calvin
    1974   " A New Look at Sect Development." *Journal for the
           Scientific Study of Religion"* 13:345-352.

Redekop, Calvin, and John A. Hostetler
    1977 "The Plain People: An Interpretation." *Mennonite
          Quarterly Review* 51:266-277.

Redekop, Calvin and Sam J. Steiner (Eds.)
    1988 *Mennonite Identity: Historical and Contemporary Per-
          spectives*. Lanham, MD.:   University Press of America.

Redekop, John
    1987 *A People Apart: Ethnicity and the Mennonite Brethren*.
          Hillsboro, KS: Kindred Press.

Richey, Russell, E. (Ed.)
    1977 *Denominationalism*. Nashville: Abingdon.

Royer, Don
    1955 "The Acculturation Process and the Peace Doctrine of
          the Church of the Brethren." Unpublished Ph.D. dis-
          sertation, University of Chicago.

Ruether, Rosemary
    1970 *The Radical Kingdom*. New York: Harper.

Sawatsky, Rodney
    1983 "Defining 'Mennonite' Diversity and Unity." *Mennonite
          Quarterly Review* 57:282-292.

Smith, Timothy
    1977 "Congregation, State, and Denomination: The Forming
          of the American Religious Structure." In Russel Richey
          (Ed.), *Denominationalism*. Nashville: Abingdon.

Swatos, William R. Jr.
    1979 *Into Denominationalism: The Anglican Metamorphosis.*
    Storrs, CT: Society for the Scientific Study of Religion.

Troeltsch, Ernst
    1960 *The Social Teachings of the Christian.* New York: Harper Torchbooks.

Troeltsch, Ernst
    1958 *Protestantism and Progress.* Boston: Beacon Hill.

Urry, James
    1988 "The Social Background to the Emergence of the Mennonite Brethren in Nineteenth Century Russia." *Journal of Mennonite Studies* 6:8-35.

Weber, Max
    1946 *From Max Weber: Essays in Sociology.* Gerth and Mills (Eds.). New York: Oxford University Press.

Weber, Max
    1958 *The Protestant Ethic and The Spirit of Capitalism.* New York: Charles Scribner's Sons.

Wilson, Bryan
    1970 *Religious Sects: A Sociological Study.* New York: McGraw-Hill.

Yinger, J. Milton
    1957 *Religion, Society and the Individual.* New York: MacMillan.

RESPONSE[1]

Thomas J. Meyers

Part of the assignment given to Calvin Redekop was to conceptualize and strategize about ways to uncover data that will help to answer the critical question of what, if anything, do late twentieth-century Mennonites have to say to the larger social order around them? Are Mennonites, in any way, sectarian like the sixteenth-century Anabaptists whose bold new vision placed them on the radical wing of the reformation? Or have Mennonites moved toward the church end of the sect-church dichotomy, and in the process lost their prophetic role in the societies in which they are found? Redekop assumes that Mennonites are assimilating. The question therefore, is not are Mennonites becoming like 'the world', but as Mennonites assimilate culturally into the mainstream do they still have distinctives that set them apart? A related and equally important question concerns structural assimilation, i.e. do Mennonites continue to have structures (principally church, family, and community) which reinforce those characteristics which are uniquely Mennonite?

Redekop suggests that the way to test the existence of a sectarian stance is to examine three basic areas: work, family, and church/community. With regard to the work or business sphere Redekop argues that we need data which will enable us to determine whether Mennonite business persons are motivated by something other than purely a profit motive or the Protestant ethic. A sectarian position might mean that Mennonite business persons' attitudes and behaviors toward wealth, charitable giving and estate planning would differ from those of non-Mennonites. More generally, he asks, do Mennonites have unique attitudes toward work which set them apart from non-Mennonites such as a sense of corporate as well as individual calling to a chosen vocation? Finally, is the world of work divided between the sacred realm of church work and the profane worlds of business and the professions? If so, what is the implication of this dualism?

Redekop treats the family as a subunit of the larger Mennonite community. He views family and congregation as the overlapping entities which form the basis of Mennonite community. He suggests that the most fruitful place to begin to analyze change in this area is to examine the explicit linkages between church and family such as the degree to which families provide leadership for the congregation or the amount of endogamy within a congregation. This line of reasoning leads to the most important point in the paper; a critique of the sole focus on members attitudes and beliefs in the first Church Member Profile.

The profile of Mennonite reality described by Kauffman and Harder in the early 1970's is based on individuals as the unit of analysis. Redekop makes the case for collecting aggregate as well as individual data. He suggests that there ought to be two units of analysis, members and congregations. Redekop argues that it is as important to know something about congregations as it is to examine individual attitudes. It is as important to have information about the role of congregational input into individual decision making such as choice of vocation, stewardship, and mutual aid practices as it is to know something about individual attitudes. If Mennonites continue to have a prophetic stance, then there ought to be ways in which congregations hold members accountable to that stance.

In the area of church life Redekop suggests that we investigate the use of professional versus lay leadership in congregations, the degree of participation in cooperative organizations, and membership loss as further indicators of the intersection between congregation and individual behavior.

The only reference that Redekop makes to the important methodological question of how to collect aggregate data is to ask outside experts to evaluate congregations. It will require more creative thinking than that to generate the kind of data that Cal is calling for. For example, suppose we selected a list of key variables such as the divorce rate, level of income, the number of single parent households, the number of teenage parents and the occupational profile of a congregation and matched this information with available census tract data for a given community. We should have some indication of differences or similarities in behaviors as well as attitudes between Mennonites and their non-Mennonite neighbors. If we are truly sectarian then there ought to be differences in these key areas.

A critique which Redekop and others have leveled against the original Church Member Profile is the use of indices of purported Mennonite values which may not actually be Mennonite but indicative of evangelical or mainline Protestant beliefs. If he is correct in this assertion then the question becomes: what would a truly Mennonite religiosity scale look like? Does Redekop have an index of piety to suggest? Such an index should indicate the ways Mennonites are critical "of secular society and of the large churches which seem too ready to tolerate the lack of spiritual discipline and commitment in their church members" (Kauffman and Harder, 1975:26). The Anabaptist scale of the original study, of course, attempts to get at a sectarian stance, including such issues as swearing of oaths, entering into litigation and nonresistance. Perhaps a more focused set of questions in areas such as vocational choice or the use and distribution of resources would enable us to more sharply delineate Mennonite beliefs and attitudes. Or at the behavioral level I would like to see an index created which would ask respondents, retrospectively, about major life choices such as the selection of a mate or a career. Items should differentiate between purely individual choices and those that were affected by the church.

Another important point that Redekop makes ought to be examined. He claims that Mennonites have not held a lot of stock in abstract values and beliefs. I think he is correct in terms of the lack of a strong theological mode but at a more pragmatic level is this the case? Beulah Hostetler has argued, in her dissertation on the Franconia Conference, that the fundamental beliefs of Mennonites "were embedded in patterns of life and were largely nonverbal in character" (quoted in Juhnke, 1988:91). To push my argument a bit further I would like to turn to the more conservative cousins of the Mennonites, the Old Order Amish.

It seems to me that in order for a group to be prophetic it must have a clear sense of not only a core set of values but of the boundary that sets the group apart from others who do not share those values. The Amish, like the Mennonites, have some difficulty when asked to succinctly articulate their beliefs and values and yet they continue to have a very clear sense of boundaries. Many non-Amish are critical of what appear to be inconsistencies between their beliefs and behaviors such as the acceptance of a ride in an automobile. To the Amish person the car or the horse and buggy is not the fundamental issue, the real concern is the boundary between the world and the church. Each time an Amish person "hitches up" or pays a "taxi" driver for a ride he or she is reminded of the difference between "them and us". The Amish are accommodating, albeit not as rapidly as Mennonites, and yet it is clear to me that they continue to be conscious of the significance of the value of boundaries, at a very pragmatic level, in maintaining an identity.

At this point in their history Mennonites have a much fuzzier notion of boundaries. The empirical questions that should be asked are both what are the values and beliefs that set them apart as well as what are the structural factors which enhance or inhibit boundary maintenance. We could use this conceptual framework to examine issues such as the rapid growth of professions among Mennonites. Mennonites are well past the stage of asking whether they should become professionals, but it would be interesting to know whether boundary questions are being asked as specialization occurs within professional categories. For example, there are many young people practicing law and medicine. The former has only recently become an acceptable vocation for a large number of Mennonites. How many congregations are helping young people o decide whether to be corporate tax lawyers versus public defenders, or plastic surgeons versus general practitioners?

The choices of public defender or general practitioner reflect a possible service motive for occupational choice, whereas the cosmetic surgeon whose job is primarily to lift or readjust sagging portions of the human form or the lawyer whose principal task is to enhance the financial position of a corporation suggest a more individualistic motivation. The question is twofold, how is the individual choice made and what impact does the church have, if any, on decision-making?

It would be interesting to know how many Mennonite professionals are described by others with the qualifier, Mennonite, as in the Mennonite lawyer, the Mennonite professor, or the Mennonite veterinarian. Bryan Wilson has argued that the mark of a true sectarian is total identification with the sect.

> The member of any of the conventional churches in western countries may not appear in his everyday life to be very different from other religiously-uncommitted or completely secular men in his life-style, morals, interest, and leisure-time pursuits. This is not true of the sectarian--he is marked emphatically by his religious allegiance, which is expected to be evident in its influence on all areas of his life. The fact that a man is a member of such and such a group-- a Mormon, a Seventh-day Adventist, or one of Jehovah's Witnesses--is in itself the single most important fact about him, telling more of what to expect of him than any other piece of information pertaining to him (Wilson, 1982:92).

It seems clear that boundaries can only be maintained if there are structures in place which reinforce those boundaries. In my own work (Meyers, 1983) with the Amish, I have argued that working in the alien environment of the RV or mobile home factory worker is not at present threatening Amish society, because the typical factory worker is still oriented much more toward his own world than that of the factory. Nearly half of my respondents who worked in factories spoke Pennsylvania German on the job. In their off work hours their time was spent almost exclusively with Amish neighbors and relatives.

In the Mennonite context it seems to me that when we begin to examine such secularizing factors as urbanization the question becomes not only what are the push and pull factors in the urban sector but what boundary maintenance structures are taken with Mennonites as they make this transition. I would like to know how many urban Mennonites spend significant portions of their time with other Mennonites? Or, in what ways are second generation urban Mennonites connected with other Mennonites of their generation. It is assumed that urbanism and individualism have gone hand in hand. Do we really know that for a fact?

The issue of whether there is anything unique or different about Mennonites of the latter part of the twentieth-century which sets them apart from mainline Protestantism is a crucial question. New research ought to help us provide an answer to this question. If the advice of Redekop is heeded, we will learn something about the dynamic relationship between congregations and members. It is my opinion that gaining insights about the structural matter, although much more difficult to get at, is as important as insights uncovered about the attitudes and beliefs of individuals.

Finally, there is a nagging question that has been raised by a number of scholars. Is it possible to generalize about Mennonites, even when the field is narrowed to North American Mennonites? In the context of this paper one might ask whether there is a Swiss/South German, Pennsylvania Dutch prophetic stance that is different than that of the descendants of Dutch/North German, Russian immigrants? Are Mennonites one cohesive group or many subgroups with a common label? There are many references in scholarly and church publications to ethnic and non-ethnic Mennonites. Redekop has argued that to use the concept of ethnicity only muddies the waters. He prefers to describe Mennonites as part of an institutionalized religious social movement; a people united by a common world view stemming from the utopian vision of the sixteenth-century (Redekop, 1988). If that is indeed the case, then there ought to be indicators of the utopian vision which cut across Mennonite subgroups. Is there something fundamentally Mennonite about mutual aid, for example, which is part of the Russian, Swiss or Hispanic Mennonite experience? New research ought to provide data which point toward the commonalities and the fundamental differences between subcategories of Mennonites.

NOTES

1 Meyers' response was made to an earlier, shorter version of Redekop's paper and is germane primarily to parts of the third section in "The Mennonite movement and the Sectarian Vision," and to parts that were omitted in the revised version.

REFERENCES

Kauffman, J. Howard and Leland Harder
1975 *Anabaptists Four Centuries Later.* Scottdale: Herald Press.

Juhnke, James C.
1988 "Mennonite History and Self-Understanding: North American Mennonitism as a Bipolar Mosaic." In Calvin W. Redekop and Samuel J. Steiner (Eds.), *Mennonite Identity.* New York: University Press of America, 83-99.

Meyers, Thomas J.
1983 *Stress and the Amish Community in Transition,* Unpublished Doctoral dissertation, Boston University.

Redekop, Calvin W.
1988 "The Sociology of Mennonite Identity: A Second Opinion." In Calvin W. Redekop and Samuel J. Steiner (Eds.), *Mennonite Identity.* New York: University Press of America, pp. 173-192.

Wilson, Bryan
1982 *Religion in Sociological Perspective.* New York: Oxford University Press.

CHAPTER 4

MODERNITY AND MODERNIZATION

Donald B. Kraybill

Modernization, modernity, modern, and modernism are slippery concepts. Their conceptual beauty lies in their ability to link vast and diverse elements of social life into a common interpretative framework. But their glory is also their doom. The sweeping analytical scope of modernization, for example, threatens to render it meaningless because its elasticity stretches over virtually everything. Historian C. Lasch argues that the term modernization is analytically bankrupt and should be discarded on the trash heap of intellectual history. Responding to Lasch, Martin Marty, Professor of the History of *Modern* Christianity--convinced that the adjective will survive as a useful intellectual tool--titled his recent four volume project *Modern American Religion* (Marty, 1986:11).

I want to identify some of the various ways the concept of modernization and its cognate terms have been used. Second, I will briefly note several studies of Anabaptist groups that have utilized the modernization framework. Third, I want to raise some methodological considerations particularly as they relate to the importance of units of analysis and methodological approaches. Fourth, I will identify some of the salient social characteristics of modernity. Finally, I will offer several suggestions for future research.

The literature on modernization, vast and voluminous, is impossible to summarize here. By 1969 Brode had compiled an annotated bibliography of the modernization literature. The stream of studies using the term has continued to grow in the past two decades. There are virtually as many definitions of the term as there are social scientists using it and the definitional problem is confounded by the fact that the term "modern" is widely used not only in the social sciences but also in history, literature, art and philosophy. The recent discussion of "post-modern," which emerged out of philosophy and the arts, adds additional ambiguity to an already murky term. The notion of modern has its roots in the thinking of the nineteenth century philosophers and social scientists who noted a fundamental shift in the nature of social life after the Enlightenment particularly as industrialization began to shape the world in new ways.

The term *modern* derives from a Latin word meaning "in this time." The English use of the word revolves around two meanings: 1) the present or contemporary moment, and 2) the era of time following medieval days. Modernization is a recent process. No modern society has a history as a modern society of more than a century and a half. And as Levy (1986:3) has noted, it has by no means been demonstrated that people can live stable lives in the face of the bizarre forms of social conduct associated with modernization.

Classical social theorists--Comte, Marx, Weber, Tonnies, Simmel and Durkheim--using various labels (Gemeinschaft und Gesellschaft, mechanical and organic solidarity, etc.) explored the social features of the modern world, asking how they differed from previous social forms and searching for the modus operandi that induced this pervasive and fundamental change. Modernization is a social *process*; whereas modernity refers to the social *features* of modern societies. Typical use of the concept of modernization reveals several salient characteristics. Modernization is comprehensive, longitudinal and societal in scope. Modernization denotes macro level, *massive* changes that occur *over time* throughout an *entire* society. The typical practice of juxtaposing modern societies against "traditional" ones is an example of what Levy (1986) calls the "fallacy of misplaced dichotomies," for it erroneously implies that modern societies lack traditions. Levy argues that it is more accurate to talk of modern and nonmodern societies.

At the outset, several assumptions deserve clarification. First, modernity should not be equated with progress. That is, modernity is not a value laden concept. Modern life in sociological perspective is not necessarily better or worse than nonmodern life. Modernity, like any other form of social organization, can be objectively analyzed and its costs and benefits can be assessed; but we ought not confer an a priori superiority on modern life. In some ways it is and in others ways it surely isn't superior to nonmodern life. Modern life, in the words of Levy, is not likely to become solitary, poor, nasty, brutish, and short. It is more likely to become crowded, affluent, nasty, brutish and long! Second, societies are not completely modern or nonmodern--there are degrees of modernity. Many aspects of nonmodern life permeate even modern societies. On some dimensions a society may be rather highly modernized while exhibiting minimal modernization in other sectors. Third, modernization can be conceptualized on two levels of social reality: *structure* and *consciousness* (Berger et. al. 1973). Thus, modernization not only revamps the social organization or social architecture of an entire society; it also penetrates our collective consciousness and alters our ways of thinking. Hence, the dimensions of modernity enumerated later in this paper can be identified and analyzed at both the structural and ideological levels. Under normal conditions, we might expect a direct relationship between the modernization of structures and the modernization of consciousness. That is, without making causal assumptions, the two dimensions of modernization can be expected under normal social conditions to rise and fall together. Under certain conditions they may function independently of one another as, for instance, when religious fundamentalists wage a sophisticated, high technology war designed to obliterate rival religious factions; or when modern nations, unable to tolerate differences, threaten to exterminate each other with nuclear weapons.

CONCEPTUALIZING MODERNITY

The conceptual waters are often muddied as cognate terms-- progress, industrialization, urbanization, development, and westernization--float alongside modernization in common parlance. These terms have more specific meanings than modernization although modernization typically encompasses many of them. Social theorists are in general agreement that the application of technology (industrialization) to vast areas of social life is the prime catalyst in the modernizing process. However, operational definitions and the empirical characteristics of modern societies vary considerably. For Lerner (1968:386) modernization is "the process of social change whereby less developed societies acquire characteristics common to more developed societies...the process of social change in which development is the economic component." With a more succinct formula that focuses explicitly on technology, Levy (1972, 1986:3) argues that modernization is simply the ratio of inanimate to animate sources of power. Berger et. al. (1973:9) define modernization as, "the institutional concomitants of technologically induced economic growth." Following Parsons, Zijderveld (1986:62) defines modernization as a "process of social-structural differentiation and a concomitant cultural generalization of values, norms and meanings." While the definitions vary in focus and nuance they underscore the role of technology in stimulating social change.

Perhaps more important for our purposes in studying Mennonites are the social features that characterize modern societies. Although the traits of modernity vary by theorist, there is considerable agreement surrounding the major creases in the face of modernity. For our purposes we might ask to what extent have these features of modernity penetrated Mennonite life--in organizational structure as well as in cultural consciousness. The following dimensions of modern life are not exhaustive nor do they follow a causal sequence. They may not all be present with the same intensity in modern societies but they do in many ways distinguish the modern world from the nonmodern one. Scholars from various disciplines accentuate different features of modern societies. Economists for instance, focus on per capita indicators--productivity, energy consumption and disposable income while historians of technology stress the impact of technological inventions.

Laying aside definitions of modernization, I want to identify then some of the characteristics of modern societies that are typically underscored by sociologists.

Differentiation. A high degree of occupational specialization produces extensive structural and functional differentiation in social institutions. The transfer of work from home to factory and office is a prime factor in the historical process. Other social activities--birth, play, education, worship and death--are also extracted from the home and become separated in place and function. Thus one might argue that modernization is essentially a process of social separation as holistic systems are separated into component parts. From divorce to mobility, from occupational specialization to the stages of death and dying; things are pulled apart and fragmented. Differentiation at the level of consciousness exhibits itself in specialized vocabularies and academic disciplines. The self is also differentiated--dichotomized into public and private roles--into multiple selves.

Pluralism. Spurred by differentiation, modern societies are characterized by a variegated matrix of diverse groups and subcultures. The ideological concomitant of pluralism is pervasive cultural relativity--fostered as competing world views collide in daily life and erode moral absolutes. From values clarification and situation ethics to contextualization in theology, relativism has penetrated modern thought. Bloom's (1987) description of cultural relativity in higher education and the negative reaction of academics to his work underscores how deeply cultural relativity is entrenched in American life.

Rationalization. For Weber, the structural expression of rationalization was the emergence of efficient bureaucracies organized around competence. At the level of consciousness, functional rationality becomes ingrained into everyday thought; means are separated from ends, and control, calculation and efficiency are highly valued. Examples include birth control, time management and the ubiquitous belief in the efficacy of science.

Functional Ties. Social relationships in the modern setting tend to be contractual, utilitarian, transitory, short term. They are what sociologists call "secondary ties." The networks of modern social ligaments revolve around separate institutional spheres and lack the overlap, density and local rootage characteristic of social ties in non-modern settings. At the cultural level long term commitments, from marriage to church affiliation, wane.

Secularization. Secularization accompanies modernization at both the structural and ideological level. Like other activities, religion becomes more specialized. At the national level the influence of religion shrinks. In the U.S. religion's separation from government is legitimated legally, of course, by the separation of church and state. On the personal level religious functions are delegated to specialized times and places. In terms of culture, belief systems become more rational, this worldly, and less oriented toward supernatural and metaphysical forces. In the modern mind, luck, chance, statistical probabilities and scientific explanations supercede the Lord's will, the guidance of the spirit and the belief in supernatural interventions in everyday life.

Futuristic. Modern societies are oriented toward the future as evinced by a widespread preoccupation with planning, strategizing, forecasting and predicting. Indeed, in the perspective of modernity, the refusal to plan is the cardinal sin. From the governmental and corporate level, to family and personal planning, the focus is on the future. Family planning, financial planning, career planning, and estate planning all illustrate the preoccupation with planning at the personal level. The ten year goals of the Mennonite church (1985-1995) represent such a modernizing trend at the denominational level.

Individuation. The individual in modern life is sharply differentiated--separated from social tribes and groups. Unlike non-modern societies, the individual in modern ones becomes the supreme reality par excellent. Identities are self constructed. Doubting the supremacy of individual rights is an unforgivable breech of morality in modern life. At the structural level, the legal apparatus of the state protects the "rights" of the individual and when it fails, the Civil Liberties Union swings into action. At the level of personal consciousness, individuation is expressed in personal achievement and personal fulfillment. Assertiveness training and the ubiquitous résumé mark the ascendancy of individuation. Japan presents a curious exception to the prominence of individuation in most modern societies. The Japanese experience suggests that individuation doesn't necessarily accompany economic and technological modernization--at least not in the early stages. Time will be the jury that determines whether or not the Japanese, over the decades, can maintain a collectivist culture in the midst of modern technology.

Abstraction. From multinational corporations to vocabulary modern things are big. Massive size is a chief structural fact of modern life. In its various forms abstraction separates the individual from the immediate, the specific, the local, the particular, and the concrete. Modernization in many ways is a process of decontextualization--as ideas, persons, and organizations are detached or separated from particular social contexts. This may be the reason some Mennonite groups resisted the use of photographs, telephones, and automobiles--all of which remove persons or conversations from highly symbolic social contexts. In any event, modern life stresses the general rather than the specific, the universal rather than the particular, and the cosmopolitan over the local. Corporate takeovers, multinational corporations and the possible merger of the two largest Mennonite bodies illustrate the modern penchant for large scale size.

Rapid Change. Modern societies welcome and thrive on change. The clock dominates modern life and modern clocks run faster than traditional ones--hence the need for time management seminars. From consumer styles to revisions on word processing documents, change pervades modern life. Social and geographical mobility as well as transitory social ties increase the liminality of social life. In other words, a great deal of modern life is lived betwixt and between--between moves, marriages, projects, children, jobs and houses.

Choice. Choice is tattooed on the fabric of modern life. Options, decisions, preferences, and choices increase dramatically in highly industrialized societies. Berger argues that modernization is a shift from fate to choice, from destiny to decision. A consequence of the rampant specialization, pluralism, and mobility, choice is endemic to modern life. From sexual preferences to life styles, from religious preferences to fast foods, from T. V. commercials to funeral options "it's *all* a matter of personal choice, since after all its *all* up to the individual." Unlike nonmodern societies, modern societies do not relieve their members from the burden of choice.

Tolerance. Prodded by diversity, pluralism, and cultural relativity, modern culture cherishes tolerance. The modern individual seeks to tolerate and to be tolerable. Dogmatism, certitude and imperialism are disdained. Values are clarified, not imposed. Moreover, values are relative and situational, not absolute. At the structural level the state protects the unique and the odd while on the personal level modern civility requires respect and tolerance for weird beliefs and unusual life styles.

Uncertainty. As a result of the foregoing, modern life is uncertain and strikingly open ended. Nonmodern life was physically uncertain due to the vagaries of weather, famine and natural disaster. By contrast, the uncertainties of modern life reside in social turbulence. Despite the enormous investment in planning and control, modern life is ironically uncertain. From the possibility of nuclear holocaust to economic collapse, tomorrow is undependable. The flux and ambiguity of the external social world coalesces with individuation to shift the search for meaning to the subjective recesses of the individual. Personal, subjective beliefs become the prime, and often only, valid source of meaningful certainty in the midst of an otherwise open-ended world.

CONCEPTUAL OVERLAP

Use of the modernization framework will likely induce some conceptual overlap. The broad scope of modernization overlaps some other theoretical orientations. I will note a few that may be of particular interest. First, the transition from *sect* to *denomination* parallels modernization. Yingers' (1970) conceptualization of sect and denomination pivots on three dimensions--bureaucratization, inclusiveness, and tolerance of societal values--all of which mirror the larger process of modernization. Whereas Yinger is interested in the nature of social ties *between* religious organizations and the larger society, modernization focuses on the larger society as a *whole*; but the variables are essentially the same. In this sense, the process of denominationalization occurs to the extent that a sectarian group is shaped by the forces of modernization at play in the larger society.

Second, as noted earlier, *individuation* typically accompanies modernization. Increasing individuation within particular religious traditions can be viewed as one dimension of social change beneath the larger canopy of modernization. At the structural level, the church's sacred wand shrinks to narrower and more specialized sectors of social life. At the level of consciousness, transcendental explanations of personal and social life erode, and lose their plausibility and efficacy. While these transformations are of particular interest to the theoreticians of secularization, they are also typically incorporated into the larger modernization framework.

Finally, the research on *assimilation* focuses on the drift of small subcultures into the cultural mainstream. However, if the cultural mainstream is a modern one, the assimilation process is essentially one of modernization. The point of all of this is that there is some conceptual overlap between other specialized theoretical perspectives and the rubric of modernization. Thus at times we may be talking about the same phenomena but using different language.

RELATED RESEARCH

I will not attempt to review the literature on modernization, an impossible task with the length constraints of this paper; however, I do want to identify several investigations of Anabaptist groups that have utilized the modernization framework. Surprisingly, relatively few scholars have used this conceptual orientation in Mennonite studies. Assimilation, church-sect, boundary maintenance, and ethnographic studies have dominated the scholarly work. Long and Blair (1976) used the modernization framework to analyze subgroup formation over several decades in the Church of the Brethren. Schlabach (1979) interpreted the Mennonite encounter with revivalism from the conceptual perspective of modernization. Olshan (1980, 1981) and Gallagher (1981) have used the concept of modernization to trace social changes among the Old Order Amish in two different settings. Jager (1984), in a particularly poor piece of work, discusses the resistance of a variety of Anabaptist groups to modernization in recent years.

In an intriguing study, covering the last century and a half, Bowman (1989) interprets social change in the Church of the Brethren under the rubric of modernization. Recently I have used the modernization umbrella to analyze Mennonite identity (Kraybill 1988) and to compare the Amish, Mennonite, and Brethren struggle with social change (Kraybill, 1987a; Kraybill and Fitzkee, 1987). I have found the conceptual framework of modernization to be useful for charting and interpreting the social history of the Old Order Amish of Lancaster County (Kraybill, 1989) as well as for my present, comparative analysis of "Amish, Mennonites and Brethren in the Quandary of Modernity." Toews (1989) discusses social change among Mennonites in the twentieth century in the context of modernity. Although many other studies have dealt with the modernization of Mennonite groups in a broad sense, they have not explicitly employed the language and categories normally associated with the modernization literature. The striking thing about virtually all of the projects cited above is that they employ a historical view-- sometimes a rather long one. Moreover their methodological approach tilts toward cultural analysis rather than quantitative analysis, and they focus on the collectivity rather than the individual as the unit of analysis.

METHODOLOGICAL CONSIDERATION

Indicators of modernization can be operationalized at several levels of social analysis to tap both consciousness and structure at each tier. Four units of analysis can be distinguished as they relate to Mennonite studies: societal, denominational, congregational, and individual. Typically, as a grand theoretical perspective, the modernization framework has been employed to trace macro changes at the *societal* level at large. Insights generated by the modernization perspective at this level can enable Mennonites to better understand the larger social world and its impact upon them. At the *denominational* level we can ask to what extent the various Mennonite denominations exhibit the features of modernity--structural differentiation, bureaucratization, tolerance, etc. On the *congregational* level of analysis we can ask to what extent modernization has penetrated the structure of consciousness of congregational units. Structural features of modernity--structural/functional differentiation, formalization, rationalization--can be readily operationalized at the congregational level. A complicating factor here is the distinction between voluntary and utilitarian organizations. Congregations, as voluntary organizations, may evolve along different paths than bureaucracies around which most of the literature revolves. Finally, at the *individual* level of analysis we can ask to what extent do individual members share a modern world view--a modern consciousness that supports individual rights, that uses rational explanations and that cherishes tolerance. While modernization has primarily been used to interpret social change on a grand societal scale, some dimensions of it can be operationalized at the individual level of analysis. In this mode the attributes of individuals rather than congregations or denominations would be tapped--behavior, attitudes, opinions, and values.

Conceptual confusion regarding levels of analysis can lead to erroneous conclusions. One example of such conceptual confusion is Olshan's (1981) argument that the Amish are modern because they make choices. His argument is based on the assumption that choice is one of, if not *the*, distinguishing characteristic of modernity. Olshan argues that the Amish are "modern" because they have acted in a modern fashion by choosing not to be modern. Even though they are not modern in many ways, they have, nonetheless, chosen not to be modern and thus because of that *choice* they are modern. They have, for instance, *decided* to build parochial schools and they have *chosen* not to own cars.

While it is true that at the collective level the Amish have made choices, Olshan's argument is muddled by two factors. First, he does not distinguish between proactive and reactive choices--between deliberate and imposed choice. Unlike moderns who welcome choice, the Amish have typically made choices by default. They have been forced to choose not to be modern. They have been reactive rather than proactive. Second and more seriously, Olshan confuses individual and organizational levels of analysis. Although the Amish have made some choices at the organizational or collective level-- many of those decisions severely restrict choice for the individual Amish person. Such restriction of individual freedom is certainly not a modern notion. Thus, while Olshan argues that the Amish show traces of modernity at the collective level, they surely are not modern in the way they restrict choice for individuals. An explicit clarification about the unit and level of analysis is essential when operationalizing modernization.

In terms of methodological procedures, the modernization perspective can be employed in several ways. Concepts can be operationalized with quantitative indicators at various levels of analysis. Such indicators can be used in one-shot cross sectional studies to compare structural units or to compare individuals. The indicators can also be used to plot social change if equivalent measures over time are available. The modernization perspective can also be utilized for interpretive, cultural analysis. Although the cultural approach is more qualitatively oriented, quantitative measures can be included to embellish the cultural analysis. In this tradition, primary attention is given to cultural data--ritual, meanings, symbols, language, and moral orders.

Wuthnow (1987) and Wuthnow et. al (1984) provide suggestive guidance for cultural analysis. Hunter (1983, 1987) used an interpretive cultural approach in his analysis of the modernization of American evangelicals. Cultural analysis can be employed in a longitudinal fashion to study social change as well as in a cross-sectional fashion. Applied to Mennonite life, interpretive cultural analysis might investigate the use of ten year goals, the rational (ends and means) vocabulary used in church growth, the wane of foot washing, the use of the lot for selecting leaders, the transformation of other ritual, and shifts in language usage, e.g., the shift from nonresistance to pacifism. The cultural approach is most fitting at the denominational or congregational level of analysis for detecting and probing the modernization of consciousness. It can also be embellished by survey data based on individual attributes.

FUTURE RESEARCH

There are several ways in which the modernization perspective might be utilized in future research. The framework of modernization can be employed as a broad interpretive paradigm for "reading" the Mennonite experience and for integrating it with other, narrower, more specific theoretical perspectives, e.g. assimilation, secularization, identity, church/sect, and boundary maintenance, etc. This can be done without attempting to operationalize particular indicators of modernity. In the absence of empirical measures, the modernization framework can serve as a useful heuristic perspective for historical and cultural interpretation.

In addition to use as a general perspective it would be beneficial to operationalize indicators of modernization for longitudinal analysis of trends in Anabaptist communities. This approach could go in two directions. A limited scale (6-10) of items could operationalize several key dimensions of modernity. Such a scale could be incorporated into research projects that focus on a variety of themes. A second approach might involve a comprehensive study of modernization using several indices of modernity. Rau (1980) offers a critical review of some possible measures.

Although modernization theory runs the risk of being abstract, macro, and general; it can provide a useful analytical perspective for understanding social change within Anabaptist related groups as well as the interaction of these groups with the dominant society.

REFERENCES

Al-Nowaihi, Mohammed
   1985 "Religion and Modernization: The General Problem of
         Islamic Responses." In Richard Rubenstein (Ed.), *Mod-
         ernization: The Humanist Response to Its Promise and
         Problems*. New York: Paragon House Publishers, 253-
         282.

Bahr, Howard M., Theodore Caplow, and Geoffrey K. Leigh
   1980 "The Slowing of Modernization and Middletown."
         Research in Social Movements, Conflicts, and Change
         3:219-232.

Bellah, R. N., et al.
   1985 *Habits of the Heart*. Berkeley and Los Angeles:
         University of California Press.

Berger, Peter L.
   1967 *The Sacred Canopy*. Garden City, NY: Doubleday.

Berger, Peter L.
   1974 *Pyramids of Sacrifice*. Garden City, NY: Doubleday.

Berger, Peter L.
   1977 *Facing Up to Modernity*. New York: Basic Books.

Berger, Peter L.
   1979 *The Heretical Imperative*. Garden City, NY: Doubleday.

Berger, Peter L., Brigitte Berger, and Hansfried Kellner
   1973 *The Homeless Mind*. New York: Random House.

Berger, Peter L., and Thomas Luckmann
   1966 *The Social Construction of Reality*. Garden City, NY:
         Doubleday.

Bibby, Reginald W.
   1979 "Religion and Modernity: The Canadian Case." *Journal
         for the Scientific Study of Religion* 18:1-17.

Bloom, Allan
1987 *The Closing of the American Mind*. New York: Simon
and Schuster.

Bowman, Carl F.
1986 "The Brethren Today." In D. F. Durnbaugh (Ed.), *The
Church of the Brethren: Yesterday and Today*. Elgin:
The Brethren Press.

Bowman, Carl F.
1989 "Beyond Plainness: Cultural Transformation in the
Church of the Brethren from 1880 to the Present,"
Volumes I and II. Unpublished Ph.D. dissertation,
University of Virginia.

Brode, J.
1969 Ed. *The Process of Modernization: An Annotated Bibliography*. Cambridge, MA: Harvard University Press.

Brown, Richard D.
1976 *Modernization: The Transformation of Ameircan Life
1600-1865*. New York: Hill and Wang.

Cultural Critique
1986-87 Special Issue: Modernity and Modernism, Post-
modernity and Postmodernism. (Winter).

Douglas, Mary
1982 "The Effects of Modernization and Religious Change." In
Mary Douglas and Stephen Tipton (Eds.), *Religion and
America: Spiritual Life in a Secular Age*. Boston:
Beacon Press, 25-43.

Dumont, Louis
1986 *Essays on Individualism*. Chicago: University of Chicago
Press.

Eisenstadt, S. N.
1966 *Modernization: Protest and Change*. New Jersey:
Prentice-Hall.

Eisenstadt, S. N.
1973 *Tradition, Change and Modernity*. New York: John Wiley
& Sons.

Ellwood, Robert S., Jr.
1987 "Modern Religion as Folk Religion." In William Nicholls (Ed.), *Modernity and Religion*. Waterloo, ON: Wilfred Laurier University Press, 19-44.

Enninger, Werner
1988 "Coping with Modernity: Instrumentally and Symbolically, with a Glimpse at the Old Order Amish." *Brethren Life and Thought* 33:154-70.

Fishman, Aryei
1983 "Judaism and Modernization: The Case of the Religious Kibbutzim." *Social Forces* 62:9-31.

Foster, George M.
1973 *Traditional Societies and Technological Change*. New York: Harper and Row.

Gallagher, Thomas E., Jr.
1981 "Clinging to the Past or Preparing for the Future? The Structure of Selective Modernization among Old Order Amish of Lancaster County, Pennsylvania." Unpublished Ph.D. dissertation, Temple University.

Grew, Raymond
1980 "More on Modernization." *Journal of Social History* 14:179-187.

Hargrove, Barbara, Ed.
1984 *Religion and the Sociology of Knowledge: Modernization and Pluralism in Christian Thought and Structure*. New York: Edwin Mellen Press.

Hunter, James Davison
1983 *American Evangelicalism*. New Brunswick, NJ: Rutgers University Press.

Hunter, James Davison
1986 "The Modern Malaise." In James Hunter and Stephen Ainlay (Eds.), *Making Sense of Modern Times: Peter L. Berger and the Vision of Interpretive Sociology*. New York: Routledge & Kegan Paul, 76-100.

Hunter, James Davison
1987 *Evangelicalism: The Coming Generation.* Chicago: University of Chicago Press.

Hunter, James Davison and Stephen C. Ainlay, Eds.
1986 *Making Sense of Modern Times: Peter L. Berger and The Vision of Interpretive Sociology.* New York: Routledge and Kegan Paul.

Jager, Edward Charles
1984 "The Anabaptists' Resistance to Modernization: A Study in the Sociology of Religious Ideas." Unpublished Ph.D. dissertation, New School for Social Research.

Kolb, David
1986 *The Critique of Pure Modernity: Hegel, Heidegger and After.* Chicago: University of Chicago Press.

Kraybill, Donald B.
1987a "At the Crossroads of Modernity: Amish, Mennonites, and Brethren in Lancaster County in 1880." *Pennsylvania Mennonite Heritage* 10:2-12.

Kraybill, Donald B.
1987b "Mennonite Woman's Veiling: The Rise and Fall of a Sacred Symbol." *Mennonite Quarterly Review* 61:298-320.

Kraybill, Donald B.
1988 "Modernity and Identity: The Transformation of Mennonite Ethnicity." In Calvin Redekop and Samuel Steiner (Eds.), *Mennonite Identity: Historical and Contemporary Perspectives.* New York: University Press of America, 153-172.

Kraybill, Donald B.
1988 *The Riddle of Amish Culture.* Baltimore: The Johns Hopkins University Press.

Kraybill, Donald B., and Donald R. Fitzkee
1987 "Amish, Mennonites, and Brethren in the Modern Era." *Pennsylvania Mennonite Heritage* 10:2-11.

Lerner, Daniel
    1968 "Modernization: Social Aspects.: In David Sills (Ed.),
          Encyclopedia of the Social Sciences, volume 10. New
          York: Macmillan and Free Press, 386-395.

Levy, Marion J., Jr.
    1972 "*Modernization: Latecomers and Survivors*. New York:
          Basic Books.

Levy, Marion J., Jr.
    1986 "Modernization Exhumed." *Journal of Developing Studies*
          2:1-11.

Long, J. Henry and Robert B. Blair
    1976 "Modernization and Subgroup Formation in a Religious
          Organization: A Case Study of the Church of the
          Brethren." *Brethren Life and Thought* 10:5-36, 69-103,
          215-232.

Loomis, Charles P. and John C. McKenney
    1963 "Introduction," In Ferdinand Tonnies, *Gemeinschaft und
          Gesellschaft*. New York: Harper and Row.

Marty, Martin E.
    1986 *Modern American Religion: The Irony of It All, 1893-1919*,
          Volume 1. Chicago: University of Chicago Press.

Mayhew, Leon
    1984 "In Defense of Modernity: Talcott Parsons and the
          Utilitarian Tradition." *American Journal of Sociology*
          89:1273-1305.

McCool, Gerald
    1985 "Freedom and Authority." In Richard Rubenstein (Ed.),
          *Modernization: the Humanist Response to Its Promise
          and Problems*. New York: Paragon House, 109-125.

Nicholls, William, Ed.
    1987 "*Modernity and Religion*. Ontario, Canada: Wilfred
          Laurier University Press.

Nicholls, William
    1987 "Immanent Transcendence: Spirituality in a Scientific
          and Critical Age." In William Nicholls, *Modernity and*

Religion. Waterloo, ON: Wilfred Laurier Universtiy Press, 167-187.

Olshan, Marc Alan
1980 "The Old Order Amish as a Model for Development." Unpublished Ph.D. Dissertation, Cornell University.

Olshan, Marc Alan
1981 "Modernity, the Folk Society, and the Old Order Amish." *Rural Sociology* 46:297-309.

Prithipaul, K. Dad
1987 "Modernity and Religious Studies." In William Nicholls (Ed.), *Modernity and Religion*. Waterloo, ON: Wilfred Laurier University Press, 131-156.

Rau, William C.
1980 "The Tacit Conventions of the Modernity School: An Analysis of Key Assumptions." *American Sociological Review* 45:244-260.

Rochberg-Halton, Eugene
1986 *Meaning Modernity: Social Theory in the Pragmatic Attitude*. Chicago: University of Chicago Press.

Roof, Wade Clark
1978 *Community and Commitment: Religious Plausibility in a Liberal Protestant Church*. New York: Elsevier North Holland.

Schlabach, Theron F.
1979 "Mennonites, Revivalism, Modernity--1683-1850." *Church History* 48:398-415.

Shils, Edward
1981 *Tradition*. Chicago: University of Chicago Press.

Smith, Huston
1987 "Can Modernity Accommodate Transcendence?" In William Nicholls (Ed.), *Modernity and Religion*, Waterloo, ON: Wilfred Laurier University Press, 157-166.

Toews, Paul
1989 "Mennonites in American Society: Modernity and the

Persistence of Religious Community." *Mennonite Quarterly Review* 63:227-246.

Von der Mehden, Fred R.
1986 *Religion and Modernization in Southeast Asia*. Syracuse, NY: Syracuse University Press.

Weber, Max
1947 *The Theory of Social and Economic Organization*. New York: Free Press.

Weiner, Myron Ed.
1966 *Modernization: The Dynamics of Growth*. New York: Basic Books.

Wellmer, Albrecht
1985 "On the Dialectic of Modernism and Postmodernism." *Praxis International* 4:337-362.

Werblowsky, R. J. Zwi
1985 "Modernism and Modernization in Buddhism." In Richard Rubenstein (Ed.), *Modernization: The Humanist Response to Its Promise and Problems*. New York: Paragon House Publishers, 283-293.

Wilson, John F.
1987 "Modernity and Religion: A Problem of Perspective." In William Nichols (Ed.), *Modernity and Religion*, Waterloo, ON: Wilfred Laurier University Press, 9-18.

Withnow, Robert
1987 *Meaning and Moral Order*. Berkeley: University of California Press.

Wuthnow, R., J. D. Hunter, A. Bergesen, and E. Kurzweil
1984 *Cultural Analysis: The Work of Peter L. Berger, Mary Douglas, Michel Foucault, and Jurgen Habermas*. Boston: Routledge and Kegan Paul.

Yinger, J. Milton
1970 *The Scientific Study of Religion*. New York: Macmillan.

Zijderveld, Anton C.
  1986   "The Challenges of Modernity." James Hunter and
         Stephen Ainlay (Ed.), In *Making Sense of Modern Times:*
         Peter D. Berger and the Vision of Interpretive Sociology.
         New York, NY: Routledge and Kegan Paul, 57-75.

RESPONSE

Beulah Hostetler

I teach in the Sociology Department of Elizabethtown College, but my training is in Religious Thought; I'm sure that influences the perspective with which I respond to Don Kraybill's paper.

In this paper, he has informed us that theories of modernity/modernization are capable of linking "vast and diverse elements into a common interpretative framework." He also observes that the terms have been employed over a wide spectrum of usage and with various meanings. He notes that in sociological usage modernization refers to a social process while modernity refers to the features of modern societies.

The interpretative framework of modernity/modernization, he notes, has been employed in a number of Anabaptist studies, including Theron Schlabach's "Mennonites, Revivalism, and Modernity, 1683-1850," published in 1979 in *Church History*, Tom Gallagher's 1981 dissertation on the Amish entitled *Clinging to the Past or Preparing for the Future*, Carl Bowman's current study of the Church of the Brethren, and a number of other published or forthcoming books and articles by Kraybill himself as listed in the bibliography of his paper. These are largely longitudinal studies employing collective rather than individual analyses.

Kraybill notes several methodological considerations relating to units of analysis and approach. Modernity/modernization, he says, tends towards analysis on the macro level, to changes that are "comprehensive, longitudinal, societal." This raises a question concerning the framework of CMP-II and whether its time span is amenable to modernity/modernization analysis. While Kraybill notes that the model might be suitably applied on the denominational level to the analysis of structures, bureaucratization, and tolerance, it is used primarily to interpret social changes on the grand scale. To illustrate, in his paper using modernity, Schlabach is dealing with 1683 to 1850, and Kraybill generally from 1880 to 1980. This leads me to ask whether CMP-II is concerned primarily with change from

1972 to 1989, and if so whether that is a reasonable span of time for the study of change.

According to Kraybill, there are certain aspects of analysis on the individual level to which modernity/modernization might be applied, e.g., the extent to which individual members share a modern world view--a modern consciousness that supports individual rights, that uses rational explanations, and that cherishes tolerance. This causes me to ask, somewhat tongue in cheek, what kind of parallels rather than contrasts there might be between sixteenth-century humanism and Anabaptist views, and compared to current Mennonite views and modernity/modernization?

Kraybill suggests that modernization concepts may be operationalized with quantative indicators in cross-sectional studies to compare structural units or individuals, to plot social change, or for interpretive cultural analysis. In the latter case he notes that "primary attention is given to cultural data, ritual, meanings, symbols, language, and moral orders." Such interpretative cultural analysis sounds promising for CMP-II. I would, however, have a word of caution (and Don and I had a little friendly disagreement over what I propose in my next few sentences here). When we ask cultural questions, we're going to get cultural answers. This is, of course, appropriate. It is not, in my opinion, subsequently appropriate to generalize from such responses and to conclude that the status of the group is primarily cultural or that cultural answers are religious answers. Although cultural expressions may have high significance for religious expressions of the group, and particularly in Anabaptist groups, if we ask cultural questions, we're going to get cultural answers. If we ask sociological questions, we're going to get sociological answers. It is not my intention to discredit the significance of social or cultural analysis. I just want us to be methodologically consistent in our conclusions.

I find intriguing Kraybill's suggestion that we might employ cultural analysis to examine the use of the Mennonite Church "Ten Year Goals," and the vocabulary used in the Church Growth movement. The examination of churchwide structures could perhaps also be included, but in the case of the Mennonite Church at least, this phenomenon belongs to the early 1970s, not the late 1980s.

I would like to ask several questions aimed more at the CMP-II project as a whole, perhaps, than at Kraybill's presentation in particular. My first question: Is CMP-II interested in charting social history, sociological variables, or religious values? How do we determine where they are the same and where they are different? In other words, when are social values and religious values the same, and when are they different?

Secondly, is change the crux of the inquiry, or is it change in terms of items that are considered of high significance?

And then finally, Kraybill has suggested several options for employing the modernity perspective in CMP-II. I would like to ask him which one he would choose and how he would employ it.

REPLY

Donald Kraybill

What I was really suggesting was that I find the modernity framework most valuable for long-term historical studies at the societal level and that I think it is more useful at the collective level than for trying to measure individual attributes. So if I were doing the study, what would I do? I would take the modernity framework as the option, using it as a large perspective to interpret a lot of the more particular data. For instance, I would take a scale like individuation very seriously, and I would hope that CMP-II could come up with a very good operational individualism scale. But then I would take that and interpret it in the larger framework of modernity, so that in my view modernity is really more of an interpretive approach for making sense out of the more particular indicators rather than a concept to be operationalized with a lot of component indicators *per se*. One could take the 1972 data and go back and reinterpret that from the different perspective of modernization. In my own work I have found it to be most helpful and valuable for that kind of analysis.

Where we have to be careful, I think, is that our time frame in CMP-II is relatively short in terms of 17 years; and my inclination would be to go with the modernity framework and use it as a way to read the Mennonite experience, and to see individualism, secularization, and sect-cycle as dimensions of this larger reality that we call modernization, so that the modernization framework would be like a skeletal framework upon which to hang some of the other pieces and that brings them together.

The other thing that I feel a little anxious about, and that you may have detected in my paper if you were reading between the lines, is that I see the modernization perspective as being particularly valuable for cultural analysis: and I suspect we're really tapping psychological attributes and beliefs in CMP-II, and our data are at the level of individual respondents. Another whole level is to look at collective documents, collective data that are peeling right off of the organization as a whole. I see the modernization perspective as being most valuable for that kind of analysis.

DISCUSSING DIALECTICAL RENEWAL

CHAPTER 5

THE SACRED AND SECULARIZATION

Peter M. Hamm

Fundamental to understanding the process of secularization is to recognize the sacred and the dialectical relationship which the two forces of sacralization and secularization generate. The discussion which follows seeks to clarify issues related to the meaning and measurement of these forces in a quest for understanding Mennonite religiosity.

ISSUES RELATED TO MEANING

Our review of the relevance of the concepts of sacralization and secularization for an analysis of Mennonite religiosity begins with a definition of religion, noting both its substantive and functional components. Certainly before we speak of religious decline, we must be clear about the nature of the system of beliefs and practices with which we are dealing.

Defining Religion

To measure the variations of religiosity which account for secularization and the opposing forces of renewal among Mennonites requires conceptual tools which are both sufficiently precise to accentuate the core or norm and sufficiently broad to embrace all conceivable beliefs and practices which represent Mennonite religiosity. Most scholars limit the term *religion* to systems of beliefs that point to the existence of the supernatural, that is, a substantive definition in terms of what religion *is*. For example James G. Fraser (1922:58) defined religion as "a belief in powers higher than man and an attempt to propitiate or please them," and Peter Berger (1974:132) explained religion as the human enterprise by which the sacred cosmos is established. Others define religion in more functional language, in terms of what religion *does*. Consequently, the definition is broad enough to include scientific humanism, Marxism, and other nonsupernatural philosophies. For example, Milton Yinger (1969:9) defined religion as a system of beliefs and practices by means of which a group of people struggles with the ultimate problems of human life. With such a definition, Yinger argues, there is no secularization, since changes are not the decline of religion but simply the development of new religious forms.

We could straddle the substantive/functionalist language by using Durkheim's (1965:62) classic definition: "A religion is a unified system of beliefs and practices relative to sacred things, that is to say, things set apart and forbidden--beliefs and practices which unite into one single moral community called a Church, all those who adhere to them." Such a definition allows for both the substantive belief in the supernatural and the more functional expression in the religious community. However useful this may appear, I recommend a strictly substantive definition for the following reasons: it will represent the popular belief held by most Mennonites and consequently facilitate more accurately the measure of its change or decline; it will establish a narrower and more definable norm of religious belief, rather than a broad definition that is difficult both to define and measure; and it will facilitate the exercise in *religious sociology* in which the tools of sociology are used for a religious end (cautioning against unwholesome change and encouraging necessary change) to be distinguished from the discipline of the *sociology of religion* which seeks simply to explain a religious phenomenon. The latter is a scientific, not a religious exercise. With such a definition of religion, we are prepared to examine some further concepts.

The Process of Sacralization

Why begin with sacralization? Logically, secularization results from the sacralized state. Chronologically, it would appear that the sacred precedes secularization. Moreover, the two processes can well be seen cyclically, since the sacralized state stimulates secularization and in the case of Max Weber's thesis of the Protestant ethic and the advanced secularized state gives rise to resacralization. In any event, before we speak of decline, transformation, or desacralization of a religious state, we must recognize the pristine state, however sacred or profane. The notion of the sacred will help to ascertain from what prior state the process of secularization has eroded the religiosity of a person, group or institution.

Whether they prefer a substantive or functionalist definition of religion, a personal belief in God or are non-believing positivists, scholars usually acknowledge the underlying premise of the sacred. For the functionalist or atheist, the sacred is perceived as an integrating mechanism of society. Those who define religion substantively, such as Berger, prefer to view religion "from within," that is, from the standpoint of *Verstehen*. In his *Rumour of Angels*, Berger (1969:70-92) speaks of "signals of transcendence," such as humanity's propensity for order, the argument from play, from hope, from damnation, and from humor. Berger (1974:132) concludes that the "reports of God's demise have been somewhat exaggerated." Keeping in mind both the substantive and functionalist definitions, Hans Mol (1976:15) explains sacralization as "the process by means of which man has preeminently safeguarded and reinforced this complex of orderly interpretations of reality, rules and legitimation." In his further explanation of the concept, Mol (1976:5) refers to sacralization as "a sort of brake applied to unchecked infinite adaptations in symbolic systems...which become increasingly more dysfunctional for the emotional security of personality and the integration of tribe and community." Hence, sacralization safeguards identity, a system of meaning, or a definition of reality; and it modifies, obstructs, or legitimates change. Moreover, it is a process rather than a mere state of sacredness. Thus, the utility of this term in analyzing change becomes apparent, for it not only includes the consolidating and stabilizing quality of setting apart, but also readily allows the dialectic in its emphasis upon process, as explained below.

Definition of Secularization

Having settled on a fairly restrictive definition of religion, we now need to give attention to a workable explanation of secularization in keeping with our understanding of religion. Derived from the Latin *saeculum,* denoting "this present age" (Cox, 1971:16), as opposed to the eternal "religious world" which is timeless, the term initially referred to the process by which a "religious" priest was transferred to parish responsibility. Later the separation of pope and emperor institutionalized such secularization through passing responsibilities from ecclesiastical to political authorities. More recently, secularization has been described as a process on the cultural level which is parallel to the political one, that is, the disappearance of religious symbols in the cultural sphere, such as freeing public schools from church control. In fact, Cox (1971:8) explains such secularization as a liberating development, "a historical process, almost certainly irreversible, in which society and culture are delivered from tutelage to religious control and closed metaphysical world views." Bryan Wilson (1985:11) observes that committed religionists confuse the evaluative and the analytical by mistaking "secularization" (the process within the social structure) for "secularism" (the ideology of those who wish to promote the decline of religion and thereby hasten the secularization process). Hence, to describe the process of secularization is not to be equated with favoring the process.

It may be useful to review the multiplicity of meanings of secularization. So rich is the word in its range of meanings and so full of internal contradictions that some scholars have proposed abandoning the concept and others have looked for an alternative. Based on a careful development of the nation through history, Bryan Wilson (1985:14) views secularization as a significant element of social change (not embracing all aspects of change) which indicates "the decline in the significance of religion in the operation of the social system, its diminished significance in social consciousness, and its reduced command over the resources (time, energy, skill, intellect, imagination, and accumulated wealth) of mankind." Wilson's understanding provides a clue for our purposes.

In his recent, helpful reflection on the secularization of Christendom, Paul Peachey (1988:45) identifies three forms: first, secularization as a shift of human endeavor from "religious" or otherworldly to "secular" or this-worldly auspices; second, secularization as the embodiment or institutionalizing of "spiritual" values in the forms of culture; and third, secularization as the "disenchantment" of the world by the gospel. In the same article, Peachey (1988:46) reminds us of Talcott Parsons' challenge not to view secularization unidimensionally as simply "a progressive decline in the 'religiousness' of the society and culture, since Christianity includes an 'inner-worldly' focus with an orientation to master over the world in the name of religious values." Hence, secularization may be defined negatively as decline or loss of other worldly or supernatural energies, but also positively as the translation of other-worldly vision into inner-worldly actions. Peachey's use of the term should encourage us to find appropriate measures of secularization, both negatively and positively.

Most useful in understanding the full range of meanings is Larry Shiner's (1967:207-20) study, "The Concept of Secularization in Empirical Research." Six types are differentiated and assessed, a summary of which follows.

1. *Decline of religion*. The previously accepted symbols, doctrines, and institutions lose their prestige and influence, culminating in a religionless society.

2. *Conformity with "this world"*. The religious group turns its

attention from the supernatural and becomes more and more interested in "this world", culminating in a total absorption in pragmatic tasks in which the religious group is indistinguishable from society.

3. *Disengagement of society from religion.* Society separates itself from religion to constitute an autonomous reality and limits religion to the sphere of private life, culminating in a purely inward religion.

4. *Transposition of religious beliefs and institutions.* Beliefs and institutions once viewed as grounded in divine power are transformed to purely human creation and responsibility, culminating in a totally anthropologized religion.

5. *Desacralization of the world.* The world is deprived of its sacred character through causal explanation and manipulation, culminating in a completely "rational" world with no supernatural phenomena.

6. *Movement from "sacred" to "secular" society.* A general concept of social change culminates in a society based on rational and utilitarian considerations.

Shiner concludes that either the concepts be dropped entirely or the term "differentiation" or "transposition" be used to incorporate the concepts expressed in points 3-5 above. Given a functionalist's definition of religion, one may need to follow Shiner's proposal.

In keeping with a substantive definition of religion, as indicated above, I propose the use of Wilson's definition of secularization as the decline in the significance of religion in the operation of the social system, which then enables us to incorporate the first two meanings described by Shiner, perhaps more in keeping with the traditional understanding of secularization and perhaps more aligned with the purpose of this analysis. However, where it serves a clear purpose and the rationale for the expansion of the definition is given, one might incorporate Shiner's three forms of differentiation. In any event, the analysis must be clear about defining and measuring the key dimensions of religious decline as most religious leaders will understand them. Only then will the analysis serve its religious purpose.

The Significance of the Dialectic

By now it is apparent that both sacralization and secularization are processes, not static concepts, and that these forces are active in a sometimes complex dialectic. In fact, it is not always apparent which is the dominant force. Peachey (1988:46) acknowledges this dialectic when he states that "paralleling the 'secularizing' trends that we can readily identify, there are also 'sacralizing' processes at work.

Old religious forms may decline, but new ones continue to emerge...'secularizing' and 'sacralizing' impulses commingle in human societies." Similarly, Harold Falding (1974:210) contrasts the synthesizing process of sacralization with the analytical process of secularization. "Secularization, through the operation of faith, builds up." Hans Mol (1976:262), with a broader definition of religion, sees a dialectic between differentiation and integration or between adaption and identity, as in the Yin/Yang dynamic, "an inexorable tendency towards conversation and integration is cross-cut by a similar inexorable tendency towards change and differentiation." In summary, there is an ongoing synthetic process of sacralization at work which accounts for the continuity of Mennonite religiosity. There is also an ongoing process of secularization which accounts for change and disruption in the religious beliefs and practices, the changes not necessarily being negative. It may well be that the interaction of these processes is necessary to avoid the rigidity of an excessively defensive stance and also to avoid total accommodation to society in which religion has lost its function. In looking for measures of both secularization and sacralization, we will need to remember that these influences do not operate independently, but may counteract and stimulate each other. An apparent loss in one measure of religiosity may well stimulate a gain in another dimension. We turn, then, to the application of these concepts to understanding Mennonite religiosity.

ISSUES RELATED TO MEASURES

One of the tests of the utility of a theoretical framework in social research is its adaptability to empirical testing. How, then, can we bridge the gap between grandiose theory and measurable indices of religiosity?

Bridging Theory and Measurement

In discovering measures of religiosity, we need to guard against losing sight of the theoretical framework we have just established. We note, first, the definition of religion we use will determine the specificity or breadth of the components included in the measures. For example, if, in keeping with a broad definition of religion, avid devotion to football or hockey is interpreted as a religious commitment (as it appears to be in some communities), then the questionnaire or instrument used will need to include such measures of one's leisure time. Secondly, we note that secularization theory will be more meaningful if the countervailing forces of sacralization are included. It is not sufficient to look only for positive and negative results of secularization. To examine the prior state or force with which secularization is in tension, we will need to look at the contemporary confessions which serve as norms against which to measure actual beliefs and practices, along with the first and sixteenth century norms of faith. Thirdly, not only do we need to account for the opposing force of sacralization, but we need also to see the forces of secularization and sacralization in dialectical tension. Thus, a particular measure of formal education can contribute both to the synthesizing force of socialization, as well as to the eroding force of relativization. Remembering this dialectic will facilitate both a careful selection of appropriate measures, as well as the appropriate interpretation of them.

Further to bridge theory with application, we need to remember that the changes in Mennonite religiosity readily fit the sacralization/secularization theory. Social analysts such as Max Weber and Ernst Troeltsch used sixteenth-century Anabaptism as an illustration of sectarian movements. Weber further demonstrated how religion can serve as an independent variable and influence economic productivity. At the same time, he identified implicit secularization in the "disenchantment of the world" (*Entzauberung*). Talcott Parsons argued that Christianity not only has an "otherworldly" dimension of religiosity, but also includes an "inner-worldly" focus or orientation to mastery over the world in the name of religious values. And Peter Berger contends that Christianity carried the seeds of the revolutionary impetus within itself, especially in social formation. In applying the theory to contemporary Mennonite religiosity, we will need to look for survivals of sixteenth-century Anabaptist asceticism--their refusal to bear arms and accept office in the service of the state, their antagonism to an aristocratic way of life, their conduct in their worldly callings, and their practice of church disciplines. At the same time, we will also need to look at the major concessions resulting from the impact of social change, which have had both a positive and negative secularizing impact.

Bridging the gap will further be achieved by learning from other social scientists who have established workable mechanisms or criteria for measuring religious dimensions. For example, Hans Mol (1976:11-13, 202-61) identified four mechanisms of sacralization--*objectification* (a projected order in the beyond), *commitment* (emotional attachment), *ritual* (worship or practice), *myth or theology* (interpretation or reality). Orrin Klapp (1969:146-80) found six criteria for "sacred sects"--enthusiasm for a central value, the element of the mystique, celebration of ritual, role of the devotee, emphasis on identity change or redemption, and solidarity of fellow-

ship or brotherhood. From her study of communes, Rosabeth
Kanter (1972:72-125) isolated six major commitment mechanisms--
sacrifice, investment, renunciation, communion, mortification, and
transcendence. And Charles Glock (1972:9-11) settled for the following dimensions of religiosity-- the *experiential* (religious emo-
tion), the *ideological* (beliefs), the *ritualistic* (religious practices), the
intellectual (information on faith tenets and sacred scriptures), and
the *consequential* (effects as seen in action). For the analysis of
Mennonite religiosity, those mechanisms will need to be chosen
which most aptly measure the forces of sacralization.

Similarly, there are attempts to trace the development and iso-
late the criteria of secularization. In their analysis of the membership of five Mennonite/Brethren-in-Christ churches in North
America, Howard Kauffman and Leland Harder (1975:298-99)
referred to the five-fold stage of re-entry or re-assimilation of Mennonites into the mainstream of society, as suggested by Karl Baehr.
Thomas O'Dea (1966:9097) saw the secularization of culture in the
following dilemmas: the *dilemma of mixed motivation* (shifting from
charismatic leadership to single-mindedness); the *symbolic dilemma*
(objection vs. alienation); the *dilemma of administrative order*
(alienation through bureaucratic structures); the *dilemma of
delimitation* (distortion of faith through concretizing it); and the
dilemma of power (voluntarism vs. coercion). No doubt, there are
other models of both sacralization and secularization, but we must
proceed to those criteria most suited to an analysis of Mennonite
religiosity.

Choosing Appropriate Measures

The utility of the above theoretical framework has been tested
by the author (1987) by applying it to Canadian Mennonite
Brethren. Measures of sacralization and secularization were
designed to interpret continuity and change over a period of one-half
century, 1925-1975. The data used included the empirical data bank
of Kauffman and Harder's (1975) Church Member Profile, their
results published in *Anabaptists Four Centuries Later*. To modify and
update the application of the theoretical framework, I am
incorporating some additional measures for both the sacralizing and
secularizing forces.

The measures of sacralization represent those social forces
which contribute to fostering Mennonite religiosity. The
Kauffman/Harder data bank supplies ample empirical evidence to
document most of the following:

1. *Factors which delineate boundaries.* These boundaries sepa-

rate the religious group from self-orientation (excessive privatization) and from the more heterogeneous social whole. The distinct separateness of Mennonites is preserved by both cognitive (the system of meaning or beliefs) and normative (personal and social ethics) boundaries, as the measures of orthodoxy and moral and social ethics indicate.

2. *Factors which enhance cohesion.* While group cohesiveness may appear to be the product of simple biological and cultural continuity, two additional factors contribute to Mennonite religiosity: family solidarity and ethnicity. Again, there is empirical data to verify these factors which enhance such cohesion.

3. *Factors which consolidate identities.* Measures which account for personal transformation into a new identity include those data relating to conversion, sanctification, devotionalism, and evangelism. Measures which identify group identity formation include data relating to religious leadership, professional and lay church ministry, and the role of women.

4. *Factors which facilitate socialization.* These include the inculcation of disciplines, learning of skills, instilling of aspirations, and teaching of social roles; and they happen through weekly participation in church activities (indicated in measures of associationalism and growth and decline of church school programs), as well as through formal instruction in educational institutions (measures reflected in attendance at private schools).

5. *Factors which reinforce integration.* To ensure retention and recruitment, the organizational structure of a religious movement both binds and preserves through its conference structure, as well as disbands and proliferates through its service agencies. The centrifugal impact of conference organization becomes apparent in the structural networks of regional, national and international levels. The centrifugal impact of conference agencies becomes apparent through the mission and service agencies, for which measures of stewardship, church agency programs, and attitudes to MCC are available.

6. *Factors which advance globalization.* Considerable progress has been achieved in establishing a global Mennonite identity, resulting from international mission and service agencies and from the intentional formation of international networks. Measures can be developed, not only to test parochial and ecumenical attitudes, but also the degree of participation in MCC, MWC, WDF, and WCC networks.

7. *Factors which restore and renew religiosity.* To restore the loss of religious vitality as a result of institutionalization and secularization, religious movements not only look back to a former

state of beliefs and practices, but allow new influences to produce revitalization. Measures can be developed which test the influences of the charismatic movement, the "signs and wonders" impact, and the electronic church, para-church agencies, and non-denominational schools. Similarly, measures can be devised which test the participation in, and impact of, revival and renewal meetings at a local church and community-wide level.

Measures of secularization represent those forces of social change which contribute specifically to religious decline, loss of faith, and "conformity to the world," in keeping with the restricted definition of secularization used in this discussion. These forces are not necessarily negative, since an apparently positive function may produce a negative effect, and vice versa. It must be remembered that the above identified sacralizing forces are simultaneously active and account for the renewal and persistence of religion despite the following erosive forces:

1. *The relativizing effect of education.* Whereas the socialization process through church participation and formal educational institutions has a sacralizing impact, it can be demonstrated through cross-tabulations and statistical correlations that there are simultaneously some relativizing consequences in the educational process. By cross-tabulating measures of education with measures of devotionalism, associationalism, general orthodoxy, fundamentalist orthodoxy, Anabaptism, and moral and social issues, it can be shown that education broadens horizons, loosens moorings, and relativizes commitment at the symbolic level.

2. *The freeing and fragmenting of urbanization.* The shift from rural to urban residence has both a positive and negative effect upon religious commitment. Along with the shift comes exposure to new ideas and the readiness to question old norms. It can, however, free one as well to choose God personally and thus strengthen the Anabaptist stance of voluntarism. Again, cross-tabulations of measures of urbanization with various components of belief and practice of Mennonite religiosity show both of the above effects of freeing and fragmenting.

3. *The challenge of occupational change.* With the shift from rurality to the urban scene, new occupations facilitate the penetration of society. The reorientation that accompanies such occupational change can have an erosive affect with the potential for religious defection, as well as the possibility of accepting the challenge to penetrate society with a Christian witness. Cross-tabulations of urban residence with measures of religious beliefs and practices, including personal and social ethics, produces a varied response.

4. *The effect of economic prosperity.* Whether or not Weber's

thesis of the influence of religion upon economic activity has a secularizing consequence can be tested empirically. Levels of income can be cross-tabulated with measures of religious beliefs and practices and personal and social ethics. Again results show both a positive and negative impact.

5. *The hazards of assimilation.* For a religious immigrant people to assume the beliefs, attitudes, and behavioral patterns of their host society may undoubtedly have a secularizing effect. Since many North American Mennonites have long since been assimilated, this criterion will apply in a greater measure to the more recent Mennonite immigrants to Canada. Measures of generational differences can be cross-tabulated with the various measures of beliefs and practices to ascertain the effect of such assimilation.

6. *The results of political involvement.* Compared to the non-participatory stance of sixteenth-century Anabaptists, Mennonites in North America today freely, although selectively, participate in the political process. The impact of such participation upon personal or group religiosity can be ascertained through measures of attitudes to church and state relationships, actual participation in political activities, the political action of the church, and the political party preferences.

7. *The impact of modernization.* Modernization impacts the North American Mennonite world not only economically, socially, and politically, but also religiously in their personal and communal lives. Measures can be formulated which test the awareness of possible and probable futures, the impact of information-age technology, the response to new economic models, alternate work-styles, and revolution in roles, the shift towards privatization and the breakdown of community, and the effect upon values, bio-ethics, leisure, etc. These measures can then be correlated with indices of religious beliefs and practices.

The above measures do not exhaust all the possible criteria of religious change and continuity. However, they do provide ample indication of the dynamics of the forces of sacralization and secularization to interpret the nature and degree of the impact of secularization upon the sacred.

SUMMATION AND CONCLUSION

For Mennonites to be concerned with secularization, *Verweltlichung*, is not a new thing. Too frequently in the past, however, the concern was registered in an alarmist fashion based on an understanding of secularization narrowly defined as conformity to the world. The above discussion has attempted to broaden the understanding of the secularization process and to show its dynamic relation to the sacred. To do so, we have retained a fairly restrictive definition of religion, as Mennonites usually have done, and explained it in terms of what religion *is*, substantively, rather than what it *does*, functionally. Moreover, we have emphasized the importance of the dynamic interaction of the two forces of sacralization, which normally builds up and shields a faith, and secularization, which usually breaks down or erodes religious commitment. At the same time, we have observed that excessive safeguarding can entrench a religious group in a needlessly defensive stance, while some aspects of the secularization process may enhance religious commitment and provide opportunities for growth. Such a theoretical framework sets the stage for identifying numerous, measurable criteria of these opposing and complementary forces.

In conclusion, we propose several suggestions for interpreting the data supplied by such measures.

1. Let us not too readily applaud high measures of religiosity, which suggest continuity in religious belief and practice, without carefully examining what is being perpetrated. Indeed, we desire the appropriate kinds of religious orthodoxy, personal and social ethics, and religious participation; but all high measures do not necessarily lead to viable religious continuity.

2. A drop in a measure of religiosity is not necessarily an unmitigated evil. Some changes simply reflect the normal process on institutionalization. Some lower indices, in another generation, may produce positive effects.

3. Interpret a significant shift in a measure, whether loss or gain, decline or advance, in the light of the larger picture. Can such significant change be anticipated? Is there a counter-vailing shift in another measure, or does the shift reinforce the beginning of a trend?

4. Remember the cyclic nature of religious renewal and decline. It is as old as Judaism of the Old Testament and represents the history of Christianity for two thousand years. And it will continue. This is not to condone indiscriminate secularization but to caution against premature conclusions about religious trends.

It is the author's observation of the Mennonite Brethren in Canada (Hamm, 1987) that where secularization encounters the sacred, the religious movement can effectively withstand change and persist in viable continuity.

REFERENCES

Berger, Peter L.
1969 *A Rumor of Angels: Modern Society and the Rediscovery of the Supernatural.* Baltimore: Penguin Books.

Berger, Peter L.
1974 "Some Second Thoughts on Substantive and Functional Definitions of Religion," *Journal for the Scientific Study of Religion* 13:125-33.

Cox, Harvey
1971 *The Secular City: Secularization and Urbanization in Theological Perspective.* New York: Macmillan.

Durkheim, Emile
1965 *The Elementary Forms of Religious Life.* Translated by Joseph Ward Swain. New York: Free Press.

Fallding, Harold
1974 *The Sociology of Religion: An Explanation of the Unity and Diversity in Religion.* Toronto: McGraw-Hill Ryerson.

Frazer, James G.
1922 *The Golden Bough.* New York: Macmillan.

Glock, Charles Y.
1973 *Religion in Sociological Perspective: Essays in the Empirical Study of Religion.* Belmont, CA: Wadsworth Publishing.

Hamm, Peter M.
1987 *Continuity and Change among Canadian Mennonite Brethren.* Waterloo: Wilfred Laurier University Press.

Kanter, Rosabeth Moss
1973 *Commitment and Community: Communes and Utopias in Sociological Perspective.* Cambridge, MA: Harvard University Press.

Kauffman, J. Howard, and Leland Harder
1975 *Anabaptists Four Centuries Later: A Profile of Five Men-*

nonite and Brethren in Christ Denominations. Scottdale, PA: Herald Press.

Klapp, Orrin E.
1969 *Collective Search for Identity.* Toronto: Holt, Rinehart and Winston.

Mol, Hans
1976 *Identity and the Sacred.* Aigincourt, ON.: Book Society of Canada.

O'Dea, Thomas F.
1966 *The Sociology of Religion.* Englewood Cliffs, NJ: Prentice Hall.

Peachey, Paul
1988 "Europe as Mission Field? Some Socio-Historical Reflections." *Mission Focus* 14:3.

Shiner, Larry
1967 "The Concept of Secularization in Empirical Research" *Journal of Scientific Study of Religion* 6:207-20.

Wilson, Bryan
1985 "Secularization: The Inherited Model." In *The Sacred in a Secular Age.* Berkeley: University of California Press.

Yinger, Milton
1969 *Religion, Society, and the Individual: An Introduction to the Sociology of Religion.* New York: Macmillan.

RESPONSE

Lawrence M. Yoder

I must begin by stating that I am not a sociologist, and I have only a passing acquaintance with the way sociologists have been working with the concepts of secularization and sacralization in measuring religious attitudes and practice. What Peter Hamm has shared with us in his paper is basically an outgrowth of his major use of the categories in his book, *Continuity and Change among Canadian Mennonite Brethren*. The definitions and approach he follows demonstrate a systematic internal coherence and yield interesting and valuable conceptual analysis.

Rather than attempt to present my reflections on his theoretical framework for the purposes of the Church Member Profile research project, I have chosen to offer some reflections on another more personal level.

I am uneasy with both the definition of religion that Hamm uses and the understanding of secularization and sacralization that he develops from it. I am uneasy with the definition of religion that excludes some of the world's great religions--Buddhism (Hinayana), Confucianism, and some forms of Hinduism, to name several. It also excludes the great modern western belief systems of Marxist dialectical materialism and capitalistic materialism, which presume the right to demand the highest loyalties and ultimately the self-sacrifice of the majority of the world's populations. Religion is about explaining why things are the way they are, how to live in the face of the realities of human existence, and to whom or what I am willing to declare my ultimate loyalty and offer my life's blood as a sacrifice.

When I think of secularization and sacralization in relation to Christian belief and life, I think in terms of images that arise out of the first chapters of Genesis. The world as God created it, before God spoke to the human beings that he had created, was alive with all manner of powers and forces, of which humans most certainly lived in awe and fear. Similar to the case among present-day animistic peoples, those first people would surely regard themselves subject to the powers and forces of the world around them. The world's multiple foci of power would most assuredly be regarded like deities that have to be placated and manipulated in order to attain and maintain some measure of security and well-being. This was a sacred world in which any false step would be a violation that would precipitate divine retribution.

It is into this world that the God of Creation spoke his liberating word to humankind, commanding people to be fruitful and multiply and rule over the world. This is a word that desacralizes the world and marks the beginning of this present *saeculum*, from which the term, secular, derives. It is God's word that secularizes the world and marks the beginning of world history, the very arena in the midst of which God reveals himself to humankind.

Living as vice-regent of the world by the word of God is what characterizes biblical faith from beginning to end. In the light of biblical faith the world is a secular, not a sacral one. Genesis 3 recounts how humans, finding themselves free from fear of the world around them, are deceived into thinking that declaring themselves free from the One who spoke to them would make them truly free-- free for a life lived without regard to any Other. This is what has been called a post-secular world, the kind of world in which radical individualism is nourished.

But humankind cannot long hide from this self-deception. At first humans of necessity take on themselves the burden of being god; and soon that dead, aspiritual, post-secular world springs to life with new forces that fill their life with fear, dread, and a multitude of unanswered questions, questions that materialistic, scientific explanation systems are powerless to answer. The world and its powers rise up, as it were, as fates to rule over humankind, this accompanied eventually by the reappearance of divination, sorcery, channeling, occult practices, drug culture, and satanic cults--a resacralized world, a new animism.

In my opinion the conceptual framework that Peter Hamm suggests for the analysis of Mennonite people is a product of an empirical frame of reference in which only a small space in the soul and a small gathering of people is reserved for God. This framework may be adaptable for some present-day forms of Christianity; but for the analysis of a movement whose very birth occasioned the break-up of the sacral world of the Constantinian synthesis of early sixteenth-century Europe, I find the choice of this conceptual framework strangely ironic.

REPLY

Peter M. Hamm

When I am asked to respond to what could be controversial points, I like to start with commonalities. This is not our first meeting, and I have learned to appreciate Larry Yoder's work in the field of missions, including a credible work in Indonesia and the writing of the history of the Indonesian Mennonite Church. There's one part of me that would respond to what he has said by replying, "Yes, I agree with you all the way." It all depends upon how you define your terms. In my paper I was laying the ground fairly comprehensively, I thought, specifying the options of choosing a rather narrow definition of religion or a very broad one, or a substantive or what sociologists know as a functional definition of religion. I suspect that the definition that Larry would prefer is the broad one in which Marxism is a religion and Mahayana Buddhism, which alleges no belief in God, is a religion; and that's surely functional for certain kinds of analyses, as long as we know what we're talking about and we're agreed in our discussion that this is the kind of definition we give to our terms.

I may appear defensive at this point, but I want to add that in my choice of a narrower definition (and I gave some reasons for it in my paper), I chose a narrower one for our CMP-II purposes here, narrower even than I used in my *Continuity and Change* book, because of the utilitarian purposes of this consultation. We want to be able to go to our churches and church members and elicit some basic information from them that will be valid, reliable, and useful for the work of the church. So I have tried here to keep to definitions of religion and secularization that they would understand and to which they would be able to respond.

On Larry's definition of secularization, there's again one part of me that goes along with him 100 percent; and again it all depends on how you define this term. If you say that God loves the world and created it, I want to believe that. In our morning devotion, when Leland Harder turned to the Scriptures for references to the concept of the world and read from John 3:16 as a reminder that God loves the world, I was wondering which verse he would choose: John 3:16 or Romans 12:1, "Be not conformed to the world." These are certainly different foci, and I would say "Let's go for the dialectic between them."

CHAPTER 6

COMMUNAL COMMITMENT AND INDIVIDUALISM

Stephen C. Ainlay

In 1985, Robert Bellah and his co-authors (Richard Madsen, William Sullivan, Ann Swindler, and Steven Tipton) published their best-selling book *Habits of the Heart* and, almost overnight, restored the interest of sociologists in the concept of individualism. I say "restored" because the issues they explore are by no means new to sociology nor intellectual inquiry more generally. Quite the contrary, the issues are certainly as old as sociology itself and, in fact, predate it by many years (a fact that Bellah, *et al.* readily acknowledge in the preface).

My remarks on individualism and commitment will center on the argument developed by Bellah and his co-authors. Given that the problem has been addressed by so many others, one might question why they are deserving of this much attention. I think one might argue, for example, that *Habits of the Heart* puts new paint (that sometimes lacks the original luster) on Riesman's (1950) thesis so ably presented in *The Lonely Crowd*. It is certainly safe to say that it fails to convey the tragic quality of individualism that one finds in the work of cultural critics--such as Christopher Lasch's *The Culture of Narcissism*. One can also point to works that have more thoroughly developed one or the other side of the tension Bellah, *et al.* treat together--notably Rosabeth Kanter's, *Commitment and Community*.

Given all this, I still believe that *Habits of the Heart* deserves our attention for a number of reasons. For one, inasmuch as it has received so much attention and created so much interest in sociology (not to mention religious studies, American studies, psychology and other fields), it will become one of those pivotal points of reference that all "thorough" research will have to acknowledge. What is more to the point, the analysis provided by Bellah and his co-authors is significant. For one thing, their treatment is new--new in the sympathetic understanding that these researchers are able to muster for the people they studied (and I think this explains a good deal of its appeal). While they do not celebrate individualism (as Adam

Smith did), neither do they seem to agonize over it (as did Weber). They argue that individualism lies at the very core of North American culture and that to abandon it would mean to abandon our deepest identity. Their complaints are not about individualism *per se* but about some of the tendencies of modern individualism that threaten to destroy it from within. Their analysis is also new in that it seeks to understand the necessary balance that must be achieved between individualism and commitment. Unlike previous analyses-- especially the work of so many recent cultural critics--they do not see individualism or commitment as solutions to the "modern dilemma" in and of themselves.

I want to raise a number of questions here, inspired by Bellah and his co-authors, that pertain to issues of Mennonite identity and our attempts to study it. Does individualism lie at the core of contemporary Mennonite identity as well? To what extent do the destructive tendencies of modern North American individualism exist within Mennonite culture? Is individualism contradictory or even inimical to Mennonite life and thought? Have Mennonites become more "individualistic?" Finally, how might we best gather information about Mennonites today that might shed further light on these and other questions related to the problem of individualism?

CONCEIVING INDIVIDUALISM

Bellah and his fellow writers never really define individualism for us. When they provide synonyms for individualism, they use the broad terms of "individual rights," "autonomy," "self-interest" and "self-reliance." While this proves frustrating to anyone wishing to operationalize the concept, it allows the authors to discuss a great many things under the rubric of individualism. Bellah (1985:30) elsewhere comes a little closer to defining what he means by individualism by asserting that "whatever else it means, individualism implies a sense of respect for the integrity and dignity of the individual person and a belief in the efficacy of the individual's action."

Fortunately, Bellah *et al.* provide a clearer notion of the forms that individualism have taken in American culture. Four forms concern them most: biblical, republican (civic), utilitarian, and expressive. The first two are regarded as more "genuine" (Bellah, *et al.* 1985:143) and the last two more pathological. In the cases of both biblical and republican individualism, the tendency of pure individualism toward the fragmenting of social life is held in check by a commitment to a shared ethical community, on one hand, and a commitment to civic participation, on the other. In the cases of utilitarian and expressive individualism, the balance between commitment and individual interest is lost; success becomes defined by economic and material gain, on the one hand, and by sheer self-gratification, on the other.

Biblical individualism and republican individualism (or civic individualism which I prefer to use here) see the individual, admittedly sacred and dignified, in relation to the larger whole, a community and a tradition. Bellah *et al.* (1985:28-9) cite the Massachusetts Bay Colony and its first governor, John Winthrop, as examples of the biblical tradition in America's past. Winthrop sought to build a community in which a genuinely ethical and spiritual life could be lived. The fortunes of the individual were not to be ignored but nor were they to be given precedence over the interests (or commitment to, from the individual's standpoint) of the ethical community. They then cite Thomas Jefferson as being equally representative of republic (civic) individualism (Bellah, *et al.*, 1985:30-1). Jefferson, they suggest, believed in the rights of the individual and the principle of political equality but argued that it could only work in a republic wherein the citizens actually participate in their own self-government. Thus while both biblical and republican (civic) forms of individualism appreciated the dignity and the rights of the individual, they also argued that these could only be maintained through a commitment to the ethical community or the republic.

By contrast to either biblical or republican individualism, utilitarian and expressive individualism (forms of "modern" individualism) focus on the self as the main form of reality and have thus created a way of life that is neither individually nor socially viable. Benjamin Franklin is offered as an example of the utilitarian individualist (Bellah, *et al.*, 1985:32-3). Franklin serves as a sort of prototype for what has since come to be described as the "American Dream"--he was born poor but attained wealth through hard work and careful calculation. The opportunity for the individual to get ahead on his or her own initiative, unhampered by constraints imposed by others, has become a basic premise of utilitarian individualism. Finally, Walt Whitman is given as an example of the expressive individualist (Bellah, *et al.*, 1985:33-5). For Whitman it is not the unhampered pursuit of material success that is important but rather the full development of a deeply feeling self and the freedom to express oneself (free of constraints and conventions). Bellah and his co-authors argue that these modern forms of individualism fail to serve the interests of community because people continually pull back from commitments to the same. Neither do these forms of individualism serve the interests of the individual. This leaves the individual particularly susceptible to anomie, alienation, and a general feeling of emptiness.

The basic thesis of *Habits of the Heart* is that the biblical and republican forms of individualism that were advocated by America's so-called "Founding Fathers" and which modulated the negative effects of pure self-interest have been replaced by utilitarian individualism (the drive for material success) and expressive individualism (the drive for self-actualization). This change in American life was by no means a cultural coincidence. With an increasing commitment to egalitarianism, a growing belief that people should rely on their "own judgment" rather than on a received authority, the emergence of the therapeutic ethos as the dominant ideology, the rise of huge bureaucratic structures, and the handing over of decision-making to bureaucratic "experts"" in more and more areas of social life, people's attachment to greater social wholes, such as ethical communities and republics, has declined. Bellah *et al.* seem to believe that American society as a whole is at a critical juncture. Americans have not yet fully yielded to modern individualism and yet most no longer have the mechanisms for fulfilling their desire to belong to a community, leaving most Americans with a deep sense of ambivalence (Bellah, *et al.*, 1985:144).

INDIVIDUALISM IN EARLY ANABAPTIST LIFE

Now the question is, does any of this have a bearing on the identity and culture of contemporary Mennonites? While Bellah and company's sojourn into America's history may seem to take us far afield, I think that their model does provide us with some useful materials for conceiving of and thinking about recent changes in Mennonite life. In order to see the model's usefulness, we need, of course, to shift our focus from North American culture to Mennonite culture.

Our beginning point must be with the question: to what extent has individualism been part of or found its way into Mennonite culture? It can be argued that individualism is deeply rooted in the Anabaptist tradition. Various writers have suggested this. C. Henry Smith (1950:21-21), in discussing the origins of Anabaptism, observed that "religion for the Brethren was a decidedly personal matter" and argued that the movement was an attempt to restore Christianity once more to a basis of personal responsibility. According to Smith (1950:21), this was evidenced in, among other things, the Anabaptist position on the interpretation of Scripture.

> While Lutherans and Reformed claimed the assistance of
> governing councils and university faculties in their inter-

pretations, and Catholics of a highly organized hierarchy
and the church fathers, the Anabaptists insisted that each
individual must decide the Bible message for himself. The
greatest degree of liberty must be granted the individual
conscience in spiritual matters. *Anabaptism was the essence
of individualism* [emphasis added].

Echoing Smith's point (while discussing pluralism rather than individualism in Mennonite history), Rodney Sawatsky (1983:283)
observes that:

> Anabaptism shared the Protestant revolt against the author-
> ity of Scripture and tradition in favor of sola Scriptura.
> Accordingly, Anabaptism embraced the fundamental prob-
> lematic of all Protestantism: whose interpretation of scrip-
> ture is authoritatively binding? Since the protestors could
> not agree on the answer to this question, a plurality of
> Protestant options quickly materialized. Despite this, the
> magisterial Reformation movements, notably the Lutheran
> and Anglican and with qualifications the Reformed as well,
> managed amazingly well to limit the segmentation of their
> particular communions. They attained this primarily by
> maintaining a notion of objective grace comparable to the
> Roman Catholic position. Anabaptism, by contrast and
> with major pluralizing implications, opted for subjective or
> individualized grace.

Whereas for most mainline reformers the Church remained "the
objective vehicle of God's grace independent of the subjective
response of the participants" (Sawatsky, 1983:283), the early
Anabaptists saw the church as the "gathering of those who have sub-
jectively responded to God's grace" (Sawatsky, 1983:284).

This early individualism within Anabaptism was undoubtedly
supplemented and refreshed by the influence of Pietism on Anabaptism during the late eighteenth and nineteenth centuries. Pietism,
with its call for the radical inward renewal of the individual, infused
Anabaptist thinking by 1800 (Schlabach 1983:224). The relationship
between Anabaptism and Pietism has been thoroughly documented
(Friedmann, 1949); and while it may not have been the driving force
behind change in the Church during the nineteenth century, it
nevertheless moved Anabaptism even closer to the Protestant view
of individual justification and forensic salvation (Schlabach, 1983).

Yet the individualism upon which Anabaptism was founded and
has maintained itself over the years was a far cry from the radical

individualism that Bellah, *et al.* decry. Robert Friedmann
(1944:122), in his discussion of Smith's book, *The Story of the Mennonites*, provided a distinction between the individualism which is
part of Mennonite tradition and that which causes Bellah *et al.* so
much cause for concern. As Friedmann (1944:122) puts it:

> Individualism can mean two different things: liberty of con-
> science (and in this sense it is accepted today by all religious
> groups even by the Roman Catholics to a certain extent--
> and is contradicted only by extreme collectivism as we expe-
> rience it in our troublesome days--), or it means independ-
> ence from one's neighbor, something which is erroneously
> so greatly overrated because it is the ideal of traditional lib-
> eralism. Between this individualism and the very different
> collectivism, we have to acknowledge several additional
> forms of living together, two of which might be relevant in
> the present context: fellowship as friendly co-operation, and
> brotherhood as a sacred concern for the brother by the true
> followers of Christ.

Friedmann argued that the driving force behind Anabaptism was this
same concern for the brother. Friedmann (1944:121) suggests that
"the central idea of Anabaptism, the real dynamite in the age of
Reformation, as I see it, was this, that one cannot find salvation
without caring for his brother, that this brother actually matters in
the personal life." This is a point that he elaborated and developed
(1949; 1950) later, and it is a position supported by others (notably
Littell, 1957; 1964).

Early Anabaptism shared traits with the "ethical community,"
with its simultaneous appreciation of the individual and the collectivity, found in the American biblical tradition celebrated by Bellah
and his co-authors. Jean Seguy (1984:207) has summarized the
vision of the Anabaptist community revealed in the Schleitheim Confession:

> The simple life, morality in individual and family behavior,
> the conformity of one's daily life to his professed beliefs,
> good will and mutual aid--all played an important role in
> the congregations. Here there could be no faith without
> good works. Brethren found guilty of grievous error,
> whether of moral shortcomings or doctrinal mistakes, were
> first confronted fraternally and then separated from the
> community if they refused to reform. In effect the con-
> gregation was the local manifestation of the Body of Christ.

If it was not pure and unified in faith and practice in its everyday reality, *individual as well as collective*, it could not celebrate communion, the symbolic expression of the unity of its members and the purity of their conduct [emphasis added].

Thus, while individualism is part of Mennonite culture it has been "moderated" by a pronounced (and perhaps even stronger) biblical tradition. Similar to Winthrop's Massachusetts Bay Colony, early Anabaptists seemed "determined to start life anew" in "company with those of like religious commitment" (Bellah, *et al.*, 1985:28). I do not want to overstate the similarities between Anabaptists and Puritans, but the point is that Anabaptism's emphasis upon individualism *and* commitment to a shared ethical community seems, like Puritan Massachusetts, to have generated a sort of biblical individualism that is quite different from the radical individualism that has been generated by its utilitarian and expressive forms. Friedmann seems to have anticipated this. As he (Friedmann, 1944:121) remarked:

> It is neither collectivism nor individualism (in the sense of independence), nor is it "mere" fellowship, that constitutes the Anabaptist Gemeinden as well as the later Mennonite groups. I would call it an essential *fellowship*, something which to a certain extent might be compared with family relations where the "I" and the "we" supplement one another. It is a group life, individual and free (as far as conscience is concerned), and yet of a kind of self-commitment which by far surpasses all sorts of pious co-devotion. And above all, it lets one forget this much advertised individualism, be it that of man's conscience or that of man's independence. In living with the brother, one does not care so much for this kind of freedom (from coercion by the group) which as a negative concept cannot be viewed as the final value of life [emphasis in orginal].

It is also possible to argue that the tradition of civic individualism runs through Mennonite history. This argument requires a somewhat greater stretching of the Bellah *et al.* thesis to Mennonite identity. Given the longstanding Mennonite posture of keeping civil government at arms-length, the Jeffersonian ideal of citizens fully participating in their self-government seems ill-suited to the Mennonite situation. As Kauffman and Harder (1975:150) observe, no other aspect of the Mennonite movement has been so thoroughly studied and documented. Still, I think that there is a sense in which

we can say that Mennonites have a long tradition of civic individualism as well as biblical individualism. If we shift our focus from
nation, state, or local government to the governance of the religious
community, this application begins to make more sense. Not only
has Anabaptism stressed the importance of the individual committed
to and fulfilling himself/herself in the brotherly order but it has also
emphasized the need for participation in the common life.

Franklin Littell (1964:94), in describing the governance prescribed by the early Anabaptists, noted that "we are confronted with a
primitive Christian brotherhood, in which each believer has his
definite role and responsibility in reaching a statement of the community decision." It was, as he pointed out, one of the first examples
of lay government in Christian history.

I think we have here the answer to one of the questions that we
posed at the outset. Individualism is not contradictory nor inimical
to Mennonite life and culture, at least not when moderated by the
biblical or civic traditions that are also part of the Anabaptist legacy.
On the other hand, radical individualism--in either its utilitarian or
expressive forms--which is excessively subjective, resulting in the
fragmentation of the group, giving the self unquestioned priority
over the collective interest of the group, is both contradictory and
inimical to Mennonite life.

MODERNITY AND CONTEMPORARY MENNONITE IDENTITY

This brings us to what is perhaps the most pressing question for
judging the applicability of the Bellah, *et al.* thesis to Mennonite life:
have the biblical and civic traditions in Mennonite culture been
weakened or replaced by utilitarian and expressive individualism?
This is an empirical question that can best be answered through
empirical study and hence part of the urgency of including a focus on
individualism in future research. Nevertheless, there have been
some changes in Mennonite life, which we can already document,
that might give us reason to believe that this shift might be occurring.

For one, we can easily document the growth of bureaucracy--
what Peter Berger, *et al.* (1983) have described as a "primary carrier"
of modernity (and accordingly, individualism). The Mennonite
Church (MC) acknowledged the proliferation of bureaucratic structures in the Church in its self-study on issues of leadership and
authority (Mennonite Church General Assembly, 1982). Most
notably this has occurred in the area of conference functions. Area
conferences in the sixteenth-century were gatherings in which
bishops and elders tried to reach agreement on moral and doctrinal

issues. Importantly, there was no ongoing organizational structure to these conferences functioning between meetings. By contrast, the district conferences of the late nineteenth and twentieth century

> began to exercise more authority among North American Mennonites. Examining and ordaining (or approving the ordination of) congregational leaders became an important conference function. The role of the conference in formulating, deciding, and implementing discipline grew. Simultaneously, conference gatherings have not been limited to ordained leaders. They have included teaching and inspirational sessions, as well as action on conference policies. In addition, many conferences have staff persons and committees which carry out the work of conference between sessions [Mennonite Church (MC) General Assembly 1982:11].

The Mennonite General Conference (MC) was added to this increasingly complex bureaucratic structure at the end of the nineteenth century. The MC General Conference itself, characteristic of bureaucracies, has become more specialized and complex, spawning a General Assembly, a General Board, and other councils and program boards.

The increasing bureaucratic quality of Mennonite life has been accompanied (as Weber would have predicted) by the proliferation of trained religious experts and the growth of the professional ministry. Harder (1983:11) suggests that, within the Central District Conference of the General Conference Mennonites (GC), the multiple lay ministry model had been all but replaced by the single salaried ministerial model by 1900. While this change has been slower in coming, it has become a trend in other branches of the Mennonite Church as well.

One can argue that the growing bureaucratic structure of and the rise of the "expert" in Mennonite churches has contributed to an increasing "bureaucratic individualism." Bellah, et al. (1985:150) briefly discuss this point, but it has been more fully developed by Alasdair MacIntyre (1981). For one, MacIntyre argues that every bureaucratic organization necessarily holds (either explicitly or implicitly) "cost effectiveness" as a criterion of its success. This is, of course, a gateway to the utilitarian type of individualism. Secondly, public decisions are turned over to the expert (in public life generally this is the manager or the therapist according to Bellah, et al.) which engenders a sort of passivity among those who would otherwise have to take responsibility for and participate in organizational decision making. More to the point here, the bureaucratic structure of the church may be replacing ethical criteria of success with utilitarian ones and the tradition of lay government may well be in the process of being replaced by an organizational structure that is sharply divided between experts (making public decisions) and others (relegated to making private decisions) despite efforts to restore the "pastor-people partnership" (Harder, 1983).

As Berger, *et al.* (1973) have pointed out, the bureaucratization of the social world has had its corresponding impact on consciousness. Not only have various social institutions become more differentiated, separated from one another, each with its proper jurisdiction, but so too has modern consciousness been divided into plural and separate spheres. This bureaucratization of consciousness has made it possible for religious individualism (Bellah *et al.*, 1985:232) to flourish in modern life.

As rural farming has become less and less characteristic of the source of livelihood pursued by most Mennonites, so too have the forces conducive to modern individualism increased. Here again we are reminded of the Jeffersonian ideal which had at its core the independent farmer who at the same time could make a living *and* participate in the common life (Bellah, *et al.* 1985:30). Jefferson lived long enough to see the decline of the independent farmer and worried that the preponderance of manufacturing occupations was leading people toward "solely making money," a change in attitude that threatened his ideal of full civic participation. The technological transformation of the marketplace, like the bureaucratization of the social world, has had its impact on consciousness. The cost-benefit analysis of the workplace becomes part of the cognitive style that is applied to other spheres of life as well. Has the well-documented shift of Mennonites away from farming to professional and technical work, management, sales, etc. (Kauffman and Harder, 1975:60; Seguy, 1984), resulted in a shift to a more utilitarian outlook? Certainly these occupational shifts demand that the question be asked.

Closely related to this issue is the tendency of people to "leave home" (Bellah, *et al.*, 1985:56). In the modern world, much of childhood and childhood socialization is preparation for leaving home. "Self-reliance" and "independence" have become the goals of "successful" parenting strategies. These child rearing strategies owe to the pursuit of careers that often involve intergenerational as well as geographic mobility. A consequence of the "career oriented" modern world has been the pursuit of professional goals over and above attachments to extended family and community. To the degree that Mennonites have become caught up in the pursuit of professional careers, it may well be that they have also accepted the fragmenting consequences. This is, of course, closely tied to issues that have been traditionally discussed under the general headings of urbanization, assimilation, professionalization, and occupational/geographic mobility.

There are a host of other features in contemporary Mennonite life which might lead us to believe that individualism is increasing. One more that I would touch on is an increasing emphasis on egalitarianism--opening the church and leadership roles to more and more people. Bellah and his co-authors (1985:143) argue (following Tocqueville's original observations on this point) that the belief in the dignity and rights of the individual has led to the proliferation of various egalitarian movements. Each of these movements has advanced the standing of previously disenfranchised groups. Ironically, the hold of community upon people has been simultaneously weakened. As the hierarchical structure of society and various relationships, which were very much a part of both the biblical and civic traditions, has declined, so too has people's willingness to grant relative authority to others or even to the institutions they represent. Thus, every individual becomes ever more free to determine what's right, what the individual should believe in as well as what standards should be upheld. Individuals become "free from" external control and constraint.

Calvin Redekop (1970) warned of the dangers that such a condition (what he terms as being "trapped in one's own subjectivity") may pose to the "free church" tradition. Redekop (1970:126) argued that:

> The deepest meaning of the free church refers, however, to that group of Christians which not only refuses to be taken in by the "mold of the world," but which is aware of its own fallibility and hence structures itself so that it can be protected from its own self-deception. The free church, therefore, is the church which not only has become aware of its own sinfulness and dependency upon God, but which has responded by obediently taking up the cross of self-denying obedience.

Redekop goes on to suggest that members of the "free" church are those who see themselves as "free to obey." His position anticipates that taken by Bellah and his co-authors, who argue that the modern notion of freedom (conceived of as "freedom from" rather than "freedom to") makes it hard to form attachments because such attachments might impinge on one's sense of being "free." Mennonites, like all others, are faced with a dilemma if Bellah and company (and Tocqueville) are to be taken seriously on this point. How does one continue to advance the rights and opportunities of all people and yet avoid the traps of subjectivity?

RESEARCH ON INDIVIDUALISM AND COMMITMENT

Only the empirical study of individualism among Mennonites today can determine whether or not these above-cited trends in Mennonite life have actually resulted in a decreased attachment and commitment to the Mennonite community and a corresponding increase in people's desire to advance their self interests (utilitarian and/or expressive). Some work has already been undertaken to try to determine this , but there is still a great need for more research.

I must admit that I am somewhat leery about how well the tension between individualism and commitment, as conceived by Bellah, et al., can be captured by the tools of survey research. It is important to remind ourselves that *Habits of the Heart* is based on empirical research so that the question is not "can it be measured?" The question is can the intricacies and the interconnectedness of a dialectical relationship--which the relationship between individualism and commitment certainly is in the biblical and civic forms--be retained, given the inevitable tendency of discrete items to artificially break down the relationships? I don't think that it is any methodological accident that Bellah and his co-authors chose to use intensive interviewing. One advantage of choosing a qualitative approach is that you are better able to capture and preserve things like "ambiguity," "ambivalence," and the like. These are key cognitive states for Bellah, et al. and I think they can best be measured qualitatively.

There are some excellent examples of just how rich the study of individualism and commitment can be when approached this way. Joseph Smucker's (1986) study of Mennonites belonging to a recently established, small church in a metropolitan area of Canada is one such example. Smucker interviewed twenty-nine people using intensive interviews. He asked questions about people's hopes and aspirations (as children, as adults, for the future), why people left rural communities, the relative importance of various things like family, the Mennonite community, identity as Mennonites, work, life style, what people desired for their children, social life outside work, and satisfaction with life as it was proceeding. From people's answers to these questions, Smucker was able to demonstrate that individualism (conceived in a manner that is very sympathetic to Bellah, et al.) has indeed made inroads into Mennonite consciousness. The urban church that he studied looks very little like the "ethical community" of biblical individualism and much more like a sort of "pit stop for emotional refueling and identity reinforcement" (Smucker 1985:284). Furthermore, Smucker documents an increasingly therapeutic quality to Mennonite life. One senses the tension, the ambivalence, and the ambiguity in the quotes Smucker uses to support his points.

Another example of the impressive empirical fruits that a qualitative approach to this problem can bear is a recent study by Leo Driedger (1982). Driedger reveals the tension between individual freedom and community control through the use of a case study approach. Using correspondence between Johann Driedger and bishops, ministers, and others, extensive correspondence, interviews with children, grandchildren, and a son-in-law, he is able to effectively demonstrate the human costs of one person's "test of the boundaries" that community provides. Like the characters we come to know in *Habits of the Heart*, you feel you know something of Johann Driedger in this work, something that may be necessary to fully come to terms with the dilemma of modern living.

There are other examples of research on non-Mennonite populations that have used content analysis to effectively reveal the issues of both individualism and commitment. Hunter (1982), for example, documents the increasing "subjectivation" of evangelical consciousness. Hunter looked at the books published by evangelical publishers that were concerned with emotional and psychological adaptions. By examining titles such as *Self-Love* and *Handbook to Happiness*, Hunter documented a sort of "psychological Christocentrism," that is, individualistic psychological well-being (rooted in a quest for self-exploration that is very much part of expressive individualism) based upon a harmonious relationship with God through Jesus Christ. Shepherd and Shepherd (1984) have also effectively used content analysis to document changing notions of commitment. They used a sample of speeches (600) that were delivered before Mormon General Assemblies between 1830 and 1930. Among other things, they were able to demonstrate how transcendental commitment--what Kanter (1972) describes as experiencing the power of community--has received the great rhetorical emphasis. It is easy to imagine similar methods being applied to the analysis of Mennonite life and, I might add, the insights that might be gained.

Each of these approaches using intensive interviewing, case study analysis, and content analysis, suggests ways in which the tension between individualism and commitment has and could be explored among contemporary Mennonites. Can the same tension be approached quantitatively? This has depended and will necessarily continue to rest on the researcher's ability to satisfactorily

operationalize individuals and commitment, as used by Bellah *et al.*
This will involve some compromise in any case.

I am afraid that most previous quantitative studies of individualism and commitment do not speak much to either side of the tension as we have conceived it here and thus are not much help to
researchers hoping to build on prior research. Studies of commitment, as applied to religion, have tended to equate it with church
attendance or some other aspect of religiosity. The more social-
psychologically oriented studies of commitment to others usually
lack an appreciation of the connection to the group. Organizational
commitment or organizational citizenship behavior as conceived by
sociologist or organization (see L. Maillet, 1984) fail to account for
the ethical component so important to community as conceived here.

Most studies of individualism (most of which use a psychological approach) are even worse than those looking at commitment.
They have tended to equate individualism with "maximizing out-
comes for the subject" (see, for example, Halpern, 1984). Those that
are presumably more sociological have tended to use indicators that
are totally unsatisfactory. Christianson (1984), for example, asked
people to indicate how important they considered various American
values and beliefs to be. Among the values that he listed was "individualism," which he equated with nonconformity. Obviously, his
sense of individualism is very different than Bellah and his co-
authors. With all the varied understandings that people have of individualism (as is evidenced in *Habits of the Heart*), this would yield
very little meaningful information. Messner's (1982) attempt to
simply equate proportion of population that is Protestant with individualism is equally (if not even more so) problematic.

There are, however, some examples of quantitative research on
individualism and commitment, some of which deal specifically with
Mennonite life, that seem more useful. One study that seems to
escape some of the weaknesses of these previous approaches is
Brodbar-Nemzer's (1986) study of Jewish ethno/religious commitment. He specifically links his work to *Habits of the Heart* and
measures social networks as well as religious participation and ritual.
To get at participation and ritual Brodbar-Nemzer used one question concerning frequency of church attendance and a scale consisting of ten Jewish rituals, ranging from those practiced by nearly all
Jews to those practiced by only the most orthodox. He tried to get
at social networks with two additional questions. He asked, "Of your
three closest friends, how many are Jewish?" Secondly, he listed a
number of factors that might make a neighborhood attractive to the
respondent and his/her household and asked, "How important is it
that a sizable number of Jews reside in the neighborhood?" Unlike

most other research into religious commitment, Brodbar-Nemzer seems to appreciate the need to take into account an ethno-community factor. A similar consideration would seem to make sense in approaching Mennonites as well. Two studies of Mennonite life using survey research methods that also provide for a broader understanding of individualism and commitment are also worth noting. Like Brodbar-Nemzer, David Appavoo's (1985) study of a community of Mennonites in Southern Ontario demonstrates the potential insights to be gained. Appavoo developed an individualism-collectivism scale and was thereby able to distinguish between people's response to the prior claims of community as opposed to their self-oriented goals. While not focusing on individualism, Howard Kauffman and Leland Harder's (1975) "communalism scale" developed for the reader in their *Anabaptists Four Centuries Later* provides a far more adequate indication of the social network dimension of ethno/religious group identity than is typical in the literature. Like Appavoo, Kauffman and Harder are able to report on the relative strength of "prior claims of the community" (measured in terms of restricted friendships, endogamy, ethnic solidarity). To a limited degree, it is possible to say that a low score on the Kauffman and Harder "communalism scale" gives some indication of individualism. For example, the questions concerning the religious background of one's spouse (aimed at establishing something about religious endogamy) are, in part, indicative of the individual's response to community claims. Appavoo (1985) uses a similar item on his individualism-collectivism scale; and Driedger, Vogt, and Reimer (1983) have used intermarriage (Mennonites to non-Mennonites) as an indirect measure (along with tolerance of dating "outsiders") of the community's diminishing hold on people.

CONCLUSION

The tension between individualism and commitment and the far-reaching implications that both have for Mennonite identity are demanding of not only new and better research but of our undivided attention more generally. In order to better make my plea for such attention, let me return to Bellah and company one more time. They (Bellah, *et al.*, 1985:144) insist that Americans face a profound impasse that must be resolved if their lives are to be "viable."

> Modern individualism seems to be producing a way of life that is neither individually nor socially viable, yet a return to traditional forms would be to return to intolerable discrimination and oppression. The question, then, is whether

the older civic and biblical traditions have the capacity to reformulate themselves while simultaneously remaining faithful to their own deepest insights.

I would argue that there is an urgency to determine whether or not Mennonites also face this "profound impasse." As I have tried to demonstrate here, I think that there is ample evidence that would lead us to believe that the social experience of contemporary Mennonites is conducive to modern individualism. Determining whether or not the impasse exists seems a necessary, and I would add, essential first step, hence the need for new and better research. If it has taken hold, then Mennonites face a profound challenge similar to that faced by contemporary American society; that is, they too will have to find means of "reformulating themselves" while "remaining faithful to their own deepest insights."

REFERENCES

Appavoo, David
  1985 "Ideology, Family and Group Identity in a Mennonite Community in Southern Ontario." *Mennonite Quarterly Review* 59:67-93.

Bellah, Robert
  1985 "Populism and Individualism." *Social Policy* 16:30-33.

Bellah, Robert, Richard Madsen, William Sullivan, Ann Swidler and Steven Tipton
  1985 *Habits of the Heart: Individualism and Commitment in American Life.* New York: Harper and Row.

Berger, Peter, Brigette Berger and Hansfried Kellner
  1973 *The Homeless Mind: Modernization and Consciousness.* New York: Random House.

Brodbar-Nemzer, Jay
  1986 "Divorce and Group Commitment: The Case of the Jews." *Journal of Marriage and the Family* 48:329-40.

Christianson, James
  1984 "Gemeinschaft and Gesellschaft: Testing the Spatial and Community Hypothesis." *Social Forces* 63:160-8.

Driedger, Leo
  1982 "Individual Freedom vs. Community Control: An Adaptation of Erickson's Ontogeny of Ritualization." *Journal for the Scientific Study of Religion* 21:226-42.

Driedger, Leo with Roy Vogt and Mavis Reimer
  1983 "Mennonite Intermarriage: National Regional and Intergenerational Trends." *Mennonite Quarterly Review* 57:132-44.

Friedmann, Robert
  1944 "On Mennonite Historiography and on Individualism and Brotherhood." *Mennonite Quarterly Review* 18:117-22.

Friedmann, Robert
  1949 "*Mennonite Piety Through the Centuries: Its Genius and*

Its Literature. Goshen, IN: Mennonite Historical Society.

Friedmann, Robert
1950 "Anabaptism and Protestantism." *Mennonite Quarterly Review* 24:12-24.

Halpern, D.
1984 "Sex, Age, and Cultural Differences in Individualism." *Journal of Genetic Psychology* 145:23-35.

Harder, Leland
1983 *The Pastor-People Partnership: The Call and Recall of Pastors from a Believer's Church Perspective.* Elkhart, IN: The Institute of Mennonite Studies.

Hunter, James D.
1982 "Subjectivation and the New Evangelical Theodicy." *Journal for the Scientific Study of Religion* 21:39-47.

Kanter, Rosabeth
1972 *Commitment and Community.* Cambridge, MA: Harvard University Press.

Kauffman, Howard and Leland Harder
1975 *Anabaptists Four Centuries Later: A Profile of Five Mennonite and Brethren in Christ Denominations.* Scottdale, PA: Herald Press.

Littell, Franklin H.
1957 "The Anabaptist Concept of Church." In Guy Hershberger (Ed), *The Recovery of the Anabaptist Vision.* Scottdale, PA: Mennonite Publishing House.

Littell, Franklin H.
1964 *The Origins of Sectarian Protestantism: A Study of the Anabaptist View of the Church.* New York: Macmillan.

MacIntyre, Alasdair
1981 *After Virtue.* Notre Dame, IN: University of Notre Dame Press.

Maillet, L.
1984 "Mowday, Steers and Porters (1979) Commitment

Questionnaire Compared to Cook and Wall's (1980) Commitment Scale." In *Psychological Reports* 55:308-315.

Mennonite Church (MC) General Assembly
1982 *Leadership and Authority in the Life of the Church: A Summary Statement.* Scottdale, PA: Mennonite Publishing House.

Messner, Steven
1982 "Societal Development, Social Equality, and Homicide." *Social Forces* 61:225-40.

Redekop, Calvin
1970 *The Free Church and Seductive Culture.* Scottdale, PA: The Herald Press.

Sawatsky, Rodney J.
1983 "Defining 'Mennonite' Diversity and Unity." *Mennonite Quarterly Review* 57:282-92.

Schlabach, Theron
1983 "Mennonites and Pietism in America, 1740-1880." *Mennonite Quarterly Review* 57:222-240.

Seguy, Jean
1984 "The French Anabaptists: Four and One-Half Centuries of History." *Mennonite Quarterly Review* 58:206-17.

Shepherd, Gary and Gordon Shepherd
1984 "Mormon Commitment Rhetoric." *Journal for the Scientific Study of Religion* 23:129-139.

Smith, C. Henry
1957 *The Story of Mennonites* (3rd Edition). Newton, KS: Mennonite Publication Office.

Smucker, Joseph
1986 "Religious Community and Individualism: Conceptual Adaptations by One Group of Mennonites." *Journal for the Scientific Study of Religion* 25:273-291.

RESPONSE

Robert Enns

Stephen Ainlay suggests that "individualism" and "commitment" are central issues in "Mennonite identity" and that in *Habits of the Heart* Robert Bellah *et al.* offer a helpful conceptual framework and an appropriate methodological approach for examining these issues. Since it is easy for me to agree with him on each of these points, I will simply offer my own version of a brief summary of the direction in which Bellah, *et al.* and Ainlay propose that we move and suggest a few additional steps which might extend our journey along that way. Some of my comments are based on my own attempt to adapt the "Church Member Profile" to Mennonites in Japan.

For Americans, according to Bellah, *et al.*, ambiguity characterizes the nature of the relationship between self and society. "Individualism" of the "utilitarian" and "expressive" varieties constitutes the "first language" which Americans utilize in explaining to others and to themselves the reasons for their choices and their actions. But North Americans also continue to speak with a "second language" of "commitments" which have been inherited from a "Biblical" and "Republican" (or "civic") past. The problem is that the historic balance between these "first" and "second languages" is being lost as the small townships in which that balance was grounded are transformed by the structural realities of corporate urban America. With the loss of the inherited "habits of the heart" which balanced individual and community interests come the dual threats of "anomie" (meaninglessness and the loss of a cultural consensus), on the one hand, and "alienation" (powerlessness in the face of various forms of despotism), on the other.

Professor Ainlay notes an analogous ambiguity in the Anabaptist tradition, in which a synthesis of voluntaristic individualism with strong communal commitments was developed. But new forms of individualism threaten the viability of this earlier Mennonite way of balancing the interests of the individual and the interests of the community. Bellah, *et al.* and Ainlay agree that these new forms of individualism are rooted in new social conditions. According to Bellah, industrialization, urbanization, the bureaucratization of the management of both private corporations and government agencies, and a compensating "therapeutic ethic" have impacted all social relationships--friendship, marriage, family and kinship, neighborhoods, workplace, religious congregation, and forms of political participation. Ainlay notes that Mennonites, like many other North Americans, are experiencing transitions into professional occupations, weaker kinship ties, and the loss of "authority" that comes with the assignment of religious leadership to professionalized "experts".

Bellah, *et al*. offer many additional concepts not cited by Ainlay which might illuminate, further, this American ambiguity in relationships between individualism and commitment. Some are familiar to sociologists and have already been incorporated into previous work (e.g., the sect to denomination transition; see Kauffman and Harder, 1975). The following concepts are less familiar but offer insights which might be useful in further study of Mennonites in America.

1. The contrast between "*community of memory*" and "*lifestyle enclave*". Bellah, *et al*. suggest that the term "community" should be reserved for groups whose identity is "constituted" by a narrative tradition. The "lifestyle enclave", in contrast, involves "segmentation" in two senses. First, only one segment (e.g. recreation, retirement, religion, or some other particular interest) of the full range of human experience forms the center for the group, and, second, only a narrow segment of the population (e.g. an age, class, ethnic, or common interest group) is represented within the membership.

Are Mennonites a "community of memory"? If so, are there elements of a Mennonite "story" without knowledge of which Mennonite identity is inconceivable? Are tales of martyrdom, migration, or mission, for example, essential to Mennonite communal identity? Familiarity with such a constitutive narrative, then, might be measured in addition to a test of Bible knowledge. (In a survey of Mennonites in Japan, for an example of an effort in this direction, members were asked to identify Menno Simons and Michael Sattler.)

Certain types of congregational insularity and homogeneity in the background and interests of members might indicate that a congregation is a segmented "lifestyle enclave" rather than a "community" in the more holistic sense suggested by Bellah, *et al*. This distinction should alert us to the possibility that agreement on beliefs and consistency in practices might be indicators of the "lifestyle enclave" rather than "community". I am not sure how this distinction might be operationalized, but I think it points to a significant issue.

2. The distinction between the "*external*" authority of both the "church" and "sect" and the "*internal*" authority of individualistic

"mysticism".   Bellah, *et. al.* suggest that the "unencumbered" self is defined by spontaneously chosen but essentially arbitrary "values" while the "constituted" self is rooted in the narrative, ritual, and organizational structures of a particular "community of memory". We might, then, want to develop some means for testing whether the convictions that an individual expresses are rooted in the "internal authority" of an "expressive individualism" or the "external authority" of commitment to a specific faith tradition. Persons might express identical beliefs or report common practices which are based upon very different sources of "authority" and which reflect, in fact, very different forms of personal identity. We might inquire, for example, whether members believe that congregational leaders or fellow members have a "right" to influence important personal decisions such as career, stewardship of financial resources, or mate selection. (E.g., Japanese Mennonites were asked to indicate whether the pastor has a responsibility in helping to arrange for the marriage of members. They were asked, also, to indicate whether they believe that the congregation or denomination has a responsibility to assist a church member during a financial crisis.)

It is apparent from what has been said already that the methods by which data are collected must be appropriate to the nature of the issues which are being investigated. Professor Ainlay notes, approvingly, that the intensive interviews which were conducted by Bellah and his associates were appropriate to the sensitive "ambiguities" which are at the center of their concerns. And he cites the work of Smucker (interviews), Driedger (biography), and Hunter (content analysis) as useful approaches to the gathering of qualitative data.

I would like to conclude my comments by suggesting two additional concerns which are related to "Mennonite identity". These concerns move beyond and complement what can be done in the "Church Member Profile" research project because they extend the boundaries of the population which is being investigated and require a methodology other than the questionnaire survey of church members.

1. *Mennonite "diaspora" and "apostates".* Driedger's (1977) metaphor of the "Mennonite ladder" might be understood in terms of a progression from communal "commitment" toward increased "individualism". The "ladder" image also raises questions about what happens to persons whose trajectory carries them *beyond* the boundaries of the Mennonite religious bodies. Where do the "diaspora" go? What do they carry with them? How do they remember what they have left behind? Takeda Kiyoka has done a sensitive study of Japanese Christian "apostates". Her work might be a suggestive con-

ceptual and methodological model for a study of North American
Mennonites who have moved beyond "home" and "church" to
destinations we know not of.

2. *Family histories*. Families differ greatly in their patterns of
transmission of religious faith across the generations. We might be
able to discern, through the construction of family histories, some of
the features of family cultures which are associated with the several
forms of "individualism" and "commitment" in Mennonite "identity".

I agree with Professor Ainlay that Bellah, *et al.*, identify issues
in American culture which help make us sensitive to possible
changes in Mennonite identity. And they provide helpful methodological models which can be useful in refining and supplementing
future surveys.

REFERENCES

Driedger, Leo
    1977 "The Anabaptist Identification Ladder: Plain-Urbane Continuity in Diversity." *Mennonite Quarterly Review* 51:278-291.

Kauffman, Howard and Leland Harder
    1975 *Anabaptists Four Centuries Later.* Scottdale, PA: Herald Press.

CHAPTER 7

IDENTITY AND ASSIMILATION

Leo Driedger

Increasingly Mennonites are turning from separation to involvement in the social networks of modern society. How can the Mennonite self be formed within a distinct identifiable group when boundaries are less obvious than in the past? How can the sacred be taught, accepted, and groomed in a secular environment? How can individualism be tempered by commitment to modern Anabaptist visions?

Our first task is to discuss theories of assimilation which predict that minorities will assimilate into or accommodate to their environment where all lose their distinctiveness in the larger melting pot. There are the pessimists who say that the majority pressures will prevail. Our second task is to focus on the characteristics of identity, group solidarity, and cohesion, which can resist these changes of secularization and modernization. The minority versus the majority and identity versus assimilation can also be seen as a dialectic of opposing forces in conflict with each other.

ASSIMILATION AND ITS MODIFICATIONS

There is a considerable debate between those who assume that the forces of secularization and modernization will draw all minorities into a melting pot of assimilation and those who believe that minorities can compete in the technological world and survive. Various theories have emerged.

Assimilation: The Melting Pot

The classical theorists--Weber, Durkheim and Marx--all agreed that the pervasive force of industrialization tends to attract workers and capitalists alike into the economic work arena where making a living becomes primary. All three agreed that industry was a major force, but they proposed different solutions as to what should be done about it. At the same time, the theory of evolution was becoming more popular, so that there was the tendency to think with Darwin and Spencer that humankind along with all other creatures was evolving to bigger and better things. Liberalism, with its stress on freedom, added to the buoyant hope that through the goodness of human beings utopia might be close at hand.

Assimilation theory suggests that immigrant groups will be synthesized into a new group. The evolutionary process it is claimed will result in a melting pot different from any of the groups involved. Americans often refer to their county as a melting pot. They broke free of British dominance 200 years ago and created a nation ostensibly dominated by no one group. All contributed to the American dream, with its new Constitution, a multitude of cultures from many parts of the world, and a system of free enterprise. Independence and freedom were popular watchwords. It was a new nation, a new culture, a new continent, a pot to which all might contribute.

A chief advocate of this interpretive process was Robert Park, who suggested that immigrants who entered America, when they came into contact with the new society, either took the route of least resistance (contact, accommodation, fusion) or a more circuitous route (contact, conflict, competition, accommodation, fusion), (Hughes, *et al.*, 1950: Shore, 1987). Whereas the latter route could take longer and entail considerable resistance on the part of the immigrant, the end result would be the same--a loss of a distinctive identity. A new culture and values would emerge.

There were a sufficient number of minorities who did assimilate, as Park predicted, to keep American researchers preoccupied with documenting the process. For fifty years, these scholars tended to ignore groups which retained a separate identity and to regard their separateness as a relatively insignificant factor in the total pattern of minority-majority relations. The assimilation theory was so influential, combined with the evolutionary thinking of the day, that it was forgotten that such well-known pluralist studies as Thomas and Znaniecki's *The Polish Peasant in Europe and America* (1918), Louis Wirth's *The Ghetto* (1928), and Harvey Zorbaugh's *The Gold Coast and the Slum* (1929), to name a few, illustrated considerable resistance to cultural pluralism, not assimilation.

The theory of assimilation was, and is, attractive because it is dynamic. It is a theory which takes into account the enormous technological change which dominates our North American societies. Furthermore, numerous studies show that many north European groups such as the Dutch, the Scandinavians, and the Germans, do fairly quickly lose many of their distinctive cultural traits such as language use. However, in the eyes of some, the theory is too deterministic. That is, as a macro theory it may explain a general process for some groups, but it does not take into account the many dimensions of change which may not be all changing in the same direction; it does not take sufficiently into account the fact that the distinctiveness of all groups may not disappear; and the targets of change may be quite different. Park's cycle does allow for some groups not to follow to the end of fusion, but the "cycle" implies that the industrial momentum will sweep everyone, some faster than others, into fusion with the general society. Park and associates did not focus very much on what was meant by fusion.

Amalgamation: Conformity to a Dominant Group

A second outcome in the process of minorities losing their traditional identity would be to join or amalgamate with another dominant and larger group. In Canada, the British represent the largest group, so we could call it Anglo-conformity. While industrialization escalated during the past several centuries, nationalism also became a close partner, which greatly influenced North American minority development as well. McNeill (1986) shows that nationalism rose in western Europe (1750-1920), especially in the most successful capitalist countries of Britain and France, which were also the most influential European players in Canada and America. The American revolution culminating in a new nation in 1776 severed colonial ties with Europe, which also freed the Americans to follow a melting pot policy. In Canada, however, first the French largely in Acadia and Quebec, and later the British (especially after the war of 1759), related to Canada in colonial terms (Breton, 1984). The influence of British nationalism and colonialism was greatly strengthened with the coming of the British Empire Loyalists to Canada.

McNeill (1986) suggests that the triumph of nationalism in Europe introduced the ideal of homogeneity within a geographic boundary and with its national sovereignty sought to bring about mono-ethnicity within its boundaries. McNeill (1986) sees this as an intrusion into the normal polyethnicity that we would normally expect in civilized industrialized countries. The British and French especially, driven by capitalist need for profits and colonization, also greatly influenced North America. The British and French fought many wars in an attempt to gain world dominance over resources, which also affected Canada especially in 1759. Later the British and French again sought to gain a monoethnic dominance in the settlement of western Canada, where the British won during the Riel rebellions of 1870 and 1885.

While monoethnic nationalism may be the most efficient way for economic capitalism to flourish with its individual enterprise, competition, and profit motive, it is for the most part in direct contradiction to other valued philosophies of political democracy and Christian religion, also an important part of western civilization. Democracy emphasizes universal suffrage and cooperation, while in Christianity brother-sisterhood, human equality, and the welfare of all is uppermost. While our economic laissez-faire capitalism may allow monoethnic dominance of one ethnos over all others, our political and religious values consider such dominance unjust.

Modified Assimilation

The two theories of minority adjustment discussed so far are basically ideal types of assimilation by which small groups give up their identity.

Milton Gordon has suggested in his *Assimilation in American Life* (1964) that assimilation is not a single social process but a number of subprocesses which he classifies under the headings "cultural" and "structural". Cultural assimilation includes acceptance by the incoming group of modes of dress, language, and other cultural characteristics of the host society. Structural assimilation concerns the degree to which immigrants enter the social institutions of the society and the degree to which they are accepted into these institutions by the majority. Gordon suggests that assimilation may occur more in the economic, political, and educational institutions, while assimilation may be resisted more in the areas of religion, family, and recreation. But, as Newman (1973) points out: "Gordon contends (that) once structural assimilation is far advanced, all other types of assimilation will naturally follow."

Gordon's multivariate approach forced scholars out of their unilinear rut. But each of the seven stages or types of assimilation he established tended to be oriented toward either an assimilationist or an amalgamationist target. Cultural, structural, marital, identificational, civic, attitudinal and behavioral receptional are viewed as seven distinctive forms of assimilation, and different ethnic groups will represent variations in the process of decline.

Gordon's major contribution is his complex multilinear, multidimensional view of the assimilation process. It has been seen as a considerable improvement on Park's assimilation cycle. Although

TABLE 1. THE SEVEN ASSIMILATION VARIABLES DEVELOPED BY GORDON

Subprocess or Condition	Type or Stage of Assimilation
Change of cultural patterns to those of host society	Cultural or behavioral assimilation
Large-scale entrance into cliques, clubs, and institutions of host society, on primary group level	Structural assimilation
Large-scale intermarriage	Marital assimilation
Development of sense of peoplehood based exclusively on host society	Identificational assimilation
Absence of prejudice	Attitude receptional assimilation
Absence of discrimination	Behavior receptional assimilation
Absence of value and power conflict	Civic assimilation

Gordon was mainly concerned with assimilation as such, and although he did not dwell on pluralism, he did not negate plural expressions in the areas of religion, the family and recreation. Application of the seven assimilation variables to minority groups like Blacks, Indians, French Canadians, and Scandinavians, for example, results in varied patterns which are most interesting. Most Blacks in Halifax, for example, as well as most American Blacks have assimilated completely culturally where their former African language, customs and religion have been lost, but they have not assimilated with respect to the last five variables where their intermarriage with whites is limited, they continue to be identifiable racially, there is considerable prejudice and discrimination against them, and they have limited access to civic power (Henry, 1972). Aboriginals in northern Canada have hardly assimilated with respect to any of the seven indicators, but this changes somewhat when they migrate into southern cities (Frideres, 1983).

On the other hand, Icelanders in Manitoba have assimilated a great deal, where few Icelandic cultural and religious institutions remain, they intermarry freely, are not very identifiable, attract little prejudice and discrimination, and some are entering places of civic influence (Driedger, 1975). Most French Canadians in Quebec, on the other hand, retain their language and culture, French institutions, marry their own kind mostly, have considerable civic power, and generally are not assimilating according to Gordon's criteria. Gordon's variables are useful because they show that individuals of some groups assimilate more than others.

IDENTITY: COUNTERVAILING FORCES

In contrast to forces of modernization, secularization, and assimilation, what are the countervailing forces of identity which Anabaptist Mennonites and BICs wish to promote? And what social pressures must they contend with in the process? The dialectic of these opposites will of course modify both in the process.

What are the dimensions and salience of identity, and what forms of identification can we find? How do some fare compared to others? Is it possible to maintain a separate identity individually, and can minority groups survive within modern society?

In his review of the literature on identity, Hans Mol (1978:1) concludes that "generally authors use 'identity' in the sense of stable niche, rather than in the sense of something to be negotiated or performed according to circumstance as the social psychologists tend to do." Wheelis (1958:200) suggests that "identity is founded...on those values which integrate and determine subordinate values." De

Levita (1965:173) thinks in a similar vein when he says that identity is "a statement of what a person or group is essentially, and as it were, permanently." Hans Mol (1978:2) likes the above definitions of identity better than social psychological ones such as Natanson's (1970) journeying self, Goffman's (1959) performing self, Berger and Luckman's (1967) role-playing self, all of which direct attention to the facade rather than to the niche-constructing self. We too regard identity as a niche, however, and are quite open to considering the importance of symbols and images which may have characteristics of performance. Identity as niche may over-stress permanence; symbols as performance allow for more process. Identity may well include features of both permanence and performance. Self or group identity may be in trouble if it becomes too much one or the other.

Peter Berger (1967:19) speaks of the socially constructed world as "an ordering of experience into a meaningful order, or *nomos*, which is imposed upon the discrete experiences and meanings of individuals." "To participate in the society is to share its 'knowledge', that is, to co-inhabit its nomos." He continues:

> The socially established nomos may thus be understood, perhaps in its most important aspect, as a shield against terror. Put differently, the most important function of society in nominization. The anthropological presupposition for this is a human craving for meaning that appears to have the force of instinct. Humans are congenitally compelled to impose meaningful order upon reality. This order, however presupposes the social enterprise of ordering world construction. To be separated from society exposes the individual to a multiplicity of dangers which we are unable to cope with ourselves.... The ultimate danger of the individual is separation from society and meaninglessness [Berger, 1967:22].

Thus, anomie (Durkheim 1954; Berger, 1967) is normlessness or life without a meaningful construct of reality.

There is the tendency for the meanings of the humanly constructed order to be projected into the universe as such, to ask the meaning of these larger more powerful sources than the historical efforts of human beings. It is at this point, Berger says (1967:25), that religion enters significantly into the argument. "Religion is the human experience by which a sacred cosmos is established. Put differently, religion is cosmization in a sacred mode. By sacred is meant here a quality of mysterious and awesome power, other than humans and yet related to us, which is believed to reside in certain objects of experience" (Berger, 1967:25). The sacred cosmos is confronted by humans as an immensely powerful reality other than ourselves. It is in this context that Hans Mol's (1976) sacralization and religious identity make sense. Mol (1976) includes objectification, commitment, ritual, and myth as important mechanisms of the construction of a religious reality, or the identification with religious phenomena, structures, and institutions. *Objectification* "is the tendency to sum up the variegated elements of mundane existence in a transcendental point of reference where they can appear more orderly, more consistent, and more timeless" (Mol, 1976:11). *Commitment* is important for emotional attachment to a specific focus of identity. *Ritual* maximizes order, reinforces the place of individuals in society, and strengthens society through repetition, emotion-provoking action, social cohesion, and personality integration. *Myth,* the fourth mechanism, is a shorthand symbolic account and celebration of a reality, through which people are related to their environment, to their ancestors, to the beyond which is the ground of all existence (Mol, 1976:13).

These mechanisms function to create a form of sacralization by means of which on the level of symbol-systems certain patterns acquire the same taken-for-granted, stable, eternal, quality which on the level of instinctive behavior was acquired by the consolidation and stabilization of new genetic materials. Sacralization, then, is a sort of brake applied to unchecked infinite adaptions, in symbol systems for which there is increasingly less evolutionary necessity and which become increasingly more dysfunctional for the emotional security of personality and for the integration of tribe or community.... Sacralization produces immunity against persuasion similar to the biological immunization process" (Mol, 1976:5). Sacralization is the inevitable process that safeguards identity when it is endangered by the disadvantages of infinite adaptability of symbol-systems. Greeley (1969:11) too hypothesizes that there is a sacralization tendency in the human condition. It is in this framework that religious identity can be discussed.

Gordon (1964:24) defines the religious or ethnic group as a group of individuals with a shared sense of peoplehood based on presumed shared sociocultural experience and/or similar physical characteristics. This includes national, linguistic, religious, and racial groups. Dashefsky (1976:8) defines group identification "as a generalized attitude involving a personal attachment to a group and a positive orientation toward being a member of a group. Therefore, identification takes place when the group in question is one with whom the individual believes he has a common ancestry based on shared individual characteristics and/or shared sociocultural experiences." Erickson suggest that, "identity is not only the sum of childhood identifications, but rather a new combination of old and new identification fragments" (1964:90).

"Identity may best be understood if it is viewed first as a higher order concept, i.e., a general organizing referent which includes a number of subsidiary facets" (Dashefsky, 1972:240). Dashefsky (1976:7) has reviewed some of the literature on identity and identification which illustrates the many dimensions of identification:

> Foote (1951) and Lindesmith and Strauss (1968) have suggested that identification involves linking oneself to others in an organizational sense (as becoming a formal member of an organization) or in a symbolic sense (as thinking of one self as a part of a particular group). Stone (1962) argues further that identification subsumes two processes: "identification of" and "identification with." The former involves placing the individual in socially defined categories. This facilitates occurrence of the latter. In Stone's terms it is "identification with" that gives rise to identity. Finally, Winch (1962:28) follows the interactionalist approach to define identification as the more or less lasting influence of one person or another. Rosen (1965:162-66) has gone further in arguing that an individual may identify with others on three levels: First, one may identify with some important person in one's life, e.g. person or a friend (i.e. significant other). Second, one may identify with a group from which one draws one's values, e.g. family or coworkers (i.e. reference group). Last, one may identify with a broad category of persons, e.g. an ethnic group or occupational group (i.e. a society category).

THEORIES OF ETHNIC IDENTITY

Sociologists and psychologists have studied identity at both macro and micro levels. Dashefsky (1975) has tried to systematize some of these macro and micro emphases, seeking to conceptualize and help operationalize future research. Dashefsky (1975) suggests that generally four frameworks (socio-cultural, interactionist, group dynamicist and psychoanalytic) have been used, the first two by sociologists, and the second two by psychologists.

Dashefsky (1975:11) classifies these four theoretical orientations along two axes shown in Table 2 using ontology (theory of reality) and methodology axes which intersect to form four cells. The first two cells deal with macro and micro sociological orientations. Sociological methods of research rely more on field study, survey research, and socio-historical analysis, while psychological methods deal a great deal with experimental and clinical studies.

TABLE 2. THEORETICAL ORIENTATION IN THE SOCIAL PSYCHOLOGY OF ETHNICITY

| | | Methodology | |
		Sociology	Psychology
Ontology	Macro-	Sociocultural	Group Dynamicist
			Psychoanalytic
	Micro-	Interactionist	Behaviorist

Source: Arnold Dashefsky, "Theoretical Frameworks in the Study of Ethnic Identity." *Ethnicity* 2:1, 1975.

The top left sociocultural cell represents a macro sociological approach in which social structure and culture are the dominant foci of identity research. In the lower left cell, the interactionist approach is more micro sociological, dealing with social psychological concern with symbols and their importance for social relationships. In the upper right cell the group dynamicist approach is a macro psychological method in which the group context is important to examine identity. The socio-cultural and the group dynamicist traditions are both macro approaches. Both look at the larger social system, but socio-culturalists stress the importance of historical experiences while group dynamicists focus more on immediate individual and group structures. The lower right cell represents the micro-psychological approach often called behaviorist, in which identity is explained in terms of reinformed responses to stimuli (Dashefsky, 1975:11). Very little research has been done in this behaviorist area of minority identity. In this paper we shall confine our theoretical review to the first two sociological macro and micro (sociocultural and interactionist) approaches. The interactionist approach was largely an attempt at rebutting the mechanistic image of humans portrayed by behaviorists. Interactionists also wanted to stress the symbolic dimensions of human behavior, which structural functionalists tended to under emphasize. The ethnocultural approach can focus so much on structures, that the dynamic features of change tend to be overly restrictive and deterministic.

The Macro Sociocultural Approach

Dashefsky (1975:12) summarized the sociocultural assumptions very well. The macro sociocultural framework assumes that individual behavior is shaped and occurs within social and cultural systems. The social system tends to define the relationships among individuals within the structure, and the cultural system defines the mutual expectations individuals share and the norms they will hold. The cultural and social system are the result of cumulated historical experiences and individual behavior is shaped within this context. The study of human behavior is more important than studying attitudes, perceptions and self-conception.

In reviewing past literature, it is clear that the multi-dimensional approach to identity has been expounded first by a host of researchers interested mostly in Jewish identity (Segalman, 1967:91-111; Geismar, 1954:33-60; Rinder, 1959:3; Adelson, 1959:457; Brenner, 1960; Lazerwitz, 1953:3-24; Janov, 1960; Anisfeld, Monoz and Lambert, 1966:31-36; Levinson, 1962:375-399; Fathi and Kinsley, 1968). Many of the factors used by Lazerwitz (1953; 1970), include some distinctly Jewish cultural items such as Zionism, although other factors such as education, religion, friendships and dating patterns could be extended to apply to any minority. The same could be said for Geismar's (1954) study of religion and Segalman's study (1967) of the General Style of Life, and Jewish Style of Life scales.

Studies show that ethnocultural identity tends to be multi-dimensional, clustering around a multiplicity of factors such as language use, religious practice, endogamy, parochial education, choice of ingroup friends, use of ethnic media and participation in ethnic voluntary organizations. Individuals and groups vary in the extent to which they emphasize different identity factors, so research needs to sort out the different factors and the patterns or profiles of ethnocultural identity.

Micro Sociological Interactionist Approach

Rose (1962) has outlined some of the major assumptions of the interactionist perspective, where he says humans live in a symbolic world, and humans are stimulated and stimulate others through symbols. Indeed, it is the ability to use symbols in a complex way which makes humans distinctive. Humans learn through symbolic communication, especially language and religion, and become reflective beings who can think abstractly, take roles, and create feelings and values. As a result humans learn to predict each others' behavior and adjust their behavior based on these predictions, and in this way define themselves in relationship to other persons and situations (Dashefsky, 1975:13). It is therefore important in identity that groups of minority individuals share symbols and their meanings and values which we often refer to as a group identification. Religious institutions, newspapers, and schools can all symbolically reinforce minority identification. Marshall Sklare (1959:20) emphasized the need to study Jewish attitudes as well as behavioral patterns. Some observers believe that there is considerable variance between the elicited responses and the actual practices of the respondents in many of the studies (Rossi, 1961:22). Lazerwitz (1953:3-24) developed three categories including behavioral, attitudinal, and conceptual categories for Jewish identification, giving most weight to behavioral items and middle weight to attitudinal items. "The decision to give more weight to behavioral than to attitudinal data is a matter for continued examination and study" (Segalman, 1967:98).

Kurt Lewin (1948) proposed that individuals need a firm clear sense of identification with the heritage and culture of their ingroup in order to find a secure basis for a sense of well being, and that insufficient ingroup security results in self-hatred and ingroup denial. Rothman's (1960:82) summary of Lewin's theory suggests that such factors as 1) self-affirmation, 2) self-denial, and 3) marginality need to be examined as independent but related variables which form, for members of a particular minority, a sense of religious or ethnic self-identity.

Many social psychologists hold that the preservation and enhancement of the self is one of the basic human needs. Segalman's extensive review of Jewish identity indicates that few scales include social psychological items. Several notable exceptions include Rothman's scale (1957), which sought to measure both positive and negative feelings toward the ingroup--feelings such as comfort, security, well-being, and self-hatred. The Geismar scale (1954:33-60) includes items related to appreciation of Jewish beliefs and rituals, and feelings of solidarity toward the Jewish community. Rinder's (1959:3) Jewish identifications scale includes items relating to pride in Jewish birth and the degree of comfort experienced in the presence of other Jews. The self-identity items of Rothman, Geismar, and Rinder appear to focus on affirmation and denial.

Lewin's theory deals with Jewish self-hatred; and the first proposition, *ethnic affirmation*, describes the extent to which members identify with the support provided by their ingroup. Are they proud of their ingroup, does it provide them with a rich heritage, do they wish to remember it or participate in it if they are given a choice? On the other hand, *ethnic denial* might include feelings and inferiority, of being restricted by and annoyed with the ingroup, or a necessity to hide their identity. *Marginality* is another concept derived from Lewin's theory, which is important in this study. Whereas, sociologically, this term has generally referred to the uncertain position of persons experiencing two cultures but identified with neither, it can also include the idea, at the psychological level, of a *discrepancy* between ingroup members' real and ideal identifications.

Having reviewed the two major sociological macro and micro perspectives on minority identity, let us discuss some of the identification factors evident in the emprical literature. We begin with three structural socio-cultural forms of identification (territory, institutions, culture), and end with three symbolic forms of identification (history, ideology, leadership). These two theoretical perspectives tend to summarize the many forms of ethnic identification on a structural-symbolic continuum, where in the middle the two approaches overlap considerably, while the respective poles are clearly distinctive ontologically and methodologically.

MINORITY IDENTIFICATION FACTORS

The writers suggests that these factors are some of the basic components that constitute Mennonite community, which Gordon (1964) referred to as a group of individuals with a shared sense of peoplehood including both structural (territory, institutions, culture) and or symbolic (history, ideology, leadership) dimensions.

Identification with a Territory

Both Joy (1972) and Lieberson (1970) argue that the maintenance of a distinctive group is not possible unless there is a sufficiently large number of the same group concentrated in a given territory. When minorities wish to develop means of control over a population in a specific area, they need to control a territory in which their offspring pass on their heritage through socialization and voluntary identification. Space becomes a crucible in which Mennonite activities take place, illustrated well in Lancaster and Waterloo counties and the rural prairie reserves and communities.

The Hutterites are one of the best examples of a rural enclavic minority community, characterized by extensive boundary mainte-nance and controlled systemic linkage with outsiders (Hostetler and Huntington, 1967). Indian reservations and Chinatowns are addi-tional examples. Rural hinterlands often contribute immigrants to the city who often perpetuate the urban villager way of life. Men-nonites have followed this trend.

Mennonite Institutional Identification

Breton (1964) argues that "the direction of the immigrant's integration will to a large extent result from the forces of attraction (positive and negative) stemming from three communities: the com-munity of the respondents' ingroup, the native (receiving) com-munity, and the other minority communities." These forces are gen-erated by the social organization of ethnic communities and their capacity to attract and hold members within their social boundaries. Minority integration into their own community, supported by institu-tional completeness of their group will reinforce solidarity.

The rationale for institutional completeness is that when a minority can develop a social system of its own with control over its institutions, the social action patterns of the group will take place largely within the system. Breton (1964) suggests that religious, educational, and welfare institutions are crucial, while Joy (1972) adds the importance of political and economic institutions. Driedger and Church (1974) found that in Winnipeg the Mennonites, French, and Jews maintained the most complete set of religious, educational, and welfare institutions compared to other minorities in the city. Residential segregation and minority institutional completeness tend to reinforce each other.

Identification with Ethnic Culture

Kurt Lewin (1948) proposed that the individual needs to achieve a firm sense of identification with the heritage and culture of the ingroup in order to find a secure "ground" for a sense of well being. We assume that a minority culture can be better groomed within the territorial enclave where an ethnic group can build a con-centration of ethnic institutions. The territory becomes a crucible within which minority institutions can be built, and the ethnic culture should flourish within these boundaries which support it.

Ethnic culture identity factors have been studied by numerous scholars from which Driedger (1975) extracted six cultural factors which differentiated group adherence to culture (language use, endogamy, choice of friends, and participation in religion, parochial schools, and voluntary organizations). French and Jewish adherents in Winnipeg ranked high on attendance of parochial schools (79 and 74 percent); endogamy (65 and 91 percent); and choice of ingroup friends (49 and 63 percent). Mennonites again ranked with the Jews and French.

Examination of territorial, institutional, and cultural structural identity factors suggest that these three tend to reinforce each other, so that when individuals of a given ethnic group identify with their ingroup along these dimensions, they tend to remain more distinctive, which blocks tendencies toward assimilation. We turn next to symbolic dimensions.

Identification with Historical Symbols

Minority rural villagers may perpetuate their social structure and community as an end in itself, without much reference to where they came from and their future purpose. A knowledge of their origins and pride in their heritage would seem to be essential for a sense of purpose and direction among minority urbanites. Without such pride and knowledge the desire to perpetuate tradition rapidly diminishes. The Jews have ritualized their history, which they place before their youth in the form of special days, fastings, candles, food habits--symbols of their past history. Such historical symbols can create a sense of belonging, a sense of purpose, a sense of continuing tradition that is important and worth perpetuating. Although tragic for the Jews, the Nazi holocaust in the 1940s and the present struggles in the Near East may be reminders of the conflict which is part of their historical past (Kallen, 1977). For Mennonites the sixteenth-century European Anabaptist persecution and the nineteenth-twentieth century Russian sagas were no less traumatic, and Mennonite Indians, Blacks, Asians, and Chicanos have their histories too.

Identification with an Ideology

A religious or political ideology can rally followers to a goal beyond (Glazer and Moynihan, 1970) cultural and institutional values. For many of the younger generation, territory, culture, and ethnic institutions seem to be means rather than an end to be perpetuated indefinitely. As urban minority groups become more sophisticated, it is doubtful that enclavic means will hold them within an ingroup orbit. A political or religious ideology, however, provides a purpose and impetus for values which are considered more important than cultural and institutional means (Bibby, 1987).

Lenski (1961) and Stark and Glock (1968) have delineated some of the dimensions of beliefs, devotionalism, ritual, associationalism and their consequences for social action. Identification with religious beliefs or a political philosophy provides a more social psychological dimension, which again asks about the meaning of this territory, these institutions, and this ethnic culture, and why should it be perpetuated or changed.

Leadership and Identification

The importance of charisma is demonstrated in a variety of new movements including Martin Luther King and Malcom X among the Blacks in the Untied States, the leadership of Rene Levesque among the Quebecois, and Harold Cardinals' Indian movement in Alberta, to name a few. Individuals with a sense of mission often adapt an ideology to a current situation, linking it symbolically with the past and using the media to effectively transform the present into a vision of the future.

Most religious movements began with charismatic leaders as demonstrated by the beginnings of the great religions (Buddha, Confucius, Abraham, Jesus, Muhammed). The importance of leadership in the early histories of the Lutherans (Martin Luther), Presbyterians (John Calvin), Mormons (Smith) and Mennonites (Menno Simons) illustrates this also. Mennonites could add recent leaders such as Harold Bender, Orie Miller, Ed Kaufman, J. B. Toews, B. B. Janz, David Toews, J. J. Thiessen, and others.

Such charismatic leaders use social psychological means of gaining a following designed to create trust with which they mold a cohesive loyalty to both leader and ingroup. They are true believers in a cause which is passed on to their followers resulting in new potential for change. Whereas in the beginning they may be less oriented to territory, institutions, culture and heritage, slowly as the movement ages such structural features become more important.

Although there may be many more dimensions with which minorities identify, we have suggested that territory, institutions, culture, heritage, ideology, and leaders are important. Studies show that different minority groups identify more with some of these dimensions than others, and some are more successful in their maintenance of a distinct community. The Hutterites are perhaps one of the most obvious groups who have survived in the rural setting, and the Jews have done so effectively in the city for centuries. The 1989 Kauffman and Harder Church Membership Profile II data show that Mennonites are almost half urban (48 percent) in North America (only 7 percent farmers). Thus, Mennonites in the city are faced with the problem of transferring from territorial and cultural identification, to ideological, historical, and institutional identification, which requires considerable reconstruction and transformation. The papers in this collection all deal with this theological and social transformation.

REFERENCES

Adelson, Joseph
1959 "A Study of Minority Group Authoritarianism." In Sklare (Ed.), *The Jews: Social Patterns of an American Group.* New York: Free Press.

Anisfeld, Moshe, Stanley Monoz and Wallace E. Lambert
1966 "The Structure and Dynamics of the Ethnic Attitudes of Jewish Adolescents." *Journal of Abnormal and Social Psychology* 66:31-36.

Bellah, Robert N.
1967 *The Sacred Canopy: Elements of a Sociological Theory of Religion.* Garden City, NY: Doubleday and Company.

Berry, J. W. *et al.*
1974 "Psychological Aspects of Cultural Pluralism: Unity and Identity Reconsidered." *Topics in Culture Learning* 2:17-22.

Bibby, Reginald
1987 *Fragmented Gods: The Poverty and Potential of Religion in Canada.* Toronto: Irwin Publishing.

Brenner, Leon Oscar
1960 "Hostility and Jewish Group Identification." Unpublished dissertation, Boston University.

Breton, Raymond
1964 "Institutional Completeness of Ethnic Communities and Personal Relations to Immigrants." *American Journal of Sociology* 70:193-205.

Dashefsky, Arnold
1975 "Theoretical Frameworks in the Study of Ethnic Identity." *Ethnicity* 2:1-15.

Dashefsky, Arnold
1976 *Ethnic Identity in Society.* Chicago: Rand and McNally.

DeLevita, Daniel J.
1967 *The Concept of Identity.* New York: Basic Books.

Driedger, Leo
    1975 "In Search of Cultural Identity Factors: A Comparison of
         Ethnic Minority Students in Manitoba." *Canadian
         Review of Sociology and Anthropology* 12:150-162.

Driedger, Leo
    1976 "Ethnic Self-Identity: A Comparison of In-Group
         Evaluations." *Sociometry* 39:131-141.

Driedger, Leo and Glenn Church
    1974 "Residential Segregation and Institutional Completeness:
         A Comparison of Ethnic Minorities." *Canadian Review
         of Sociology and Anthropology* 11:30-52.

Durkheim, Emile
    1954 *The Elementary Forms of Religious Life.* Glencoe, IL:
         Free Press.

Fathi, Asghar and Brian L. Kinsley
    1968 "The Changing Identity of Jewish Youth in Canada."
         Paper presented at the Canadian Sociology and
         Anthropology Association meetings.

Foote, Nelson
    1951 "Identification as the Basis for a Theory of Motivation."
         American Sociological Review 15:14-21.

Frideres, James
    1983 *Native People in Canada: Contemporary Conflicts.* Scar-
         borough, ON: Prentice-Hall Canada.

Geismar, Ludwig
    1954 "A Scale for the Measurement of Ethnic Identification."
         Jewish Social Studies 16:33-60.

Glazer, Nathan and Daniel P. Moynihan
    1970 *Beyond the Melting Pot.* Cambridge, MA: M.I.T.

Goffman, E.
    1959 *The Presentation of Self in Everyday Life.* Garden City,
         NY: Doubleday.

Gordon, Milton
    1964 *Assimilation in American Life.* New York: Oxford University Press.

Greeley, Andrew
    1969 *Religion in the Year 2000.* New York: Sheed and Ward.

Henry, Frances
    1973 *Forgotten Canadians: The Blacks of Nova Scotia.* Don Mills, ON: Longman Canada.

Hughes, Everett C., *et al.* (Eds.)
    1950 *Race and Culture.* Volume 1. The Collected Papers of Robert Ezra Park. Glencoe, IL: Free Press.

Isajiw, Wsevolod W.
    1981 "Ethnic Identity Retention." Research Paper No. 125. Toronto: Centre for Urban and Community Affairs Studies.

Isajiw, Wsevolod W. and Leo Driedger
    1987 "Ethnic Identity: Resource or Drawback for Social Mobility?" Paper presented at the American Sociological meetings in Chicago.

Janov, Arthur
    1960 "A Study of Differences of the Polarities of Jewish Identification." Unpublished dissertation, Claremont Graduate School.

Joy, Richard J.
    1972 *Languages in Conflict.* Toronto: McClelland and Stewart.

Kallen, Evelyn
    1977 *Spanning the Generations: A Study in Jewish Identity.* Don Mills, ON: Longmans.

Kauffman, J. Howard and Leland Harder
    1975 *Anabaptists Four Centuries Later.* Scottdale, PA: Herald Press.

Lazerwitz, Bernard
  1953 "Some Factors in Jewish Identification." *Jewish Social Studies* 15:24.

Lazerwitz, Bernard
  1970 "An Approach to the Components and Consequences of Religio-Ethnic Identification." Unpublished manuscript.

Lenski, Gerhard
  1961 *The Religious Factor.* Garden City, NY: Doubleday Company.

Levinson, B.M.
  1962 "Yeshiva College Sub-Cultural Scale: An Experimental Attempt to Devise Scale of the Internalization of Jewish Traditional Values." *Journal of Genetic Psychology* 101:375-399.

Lewin, Kurt
  1948 *Resolving Social Conflicts.* New York: Harper and Brothers.

Lieberson, Stanley
  1970 *Languages and Ethnic Relations in Canada.* New York: John Wiley.

Lindesmith, Alfred and A. L. Strauss
  1968 *Social Psychology* (3rd edition). New York: Holt, Rinehart and Winston.

McNeill, William H.
  1986 *Poly-Ethnicity and National Unity in World History.* Toronto: University of Toronto Press.

Mol, Hans
  1976 *Identity and the Sacred.* Agincourt, ON: Book Society of Canada.

Mol, Hans
  1978 *Identity and Religion: International, Cross-Cultural Approaches.* London: Sage Publications.

Nahirney, Vladimir and Joshua A. Fishman
  1967 "American Immigrant Groups: Ethnic Identification and

the Problem of Generations." *Sociological Review* 13:311-326.

Natanson, Maurice
1970 *The Journeying Self.* Reading, Massachusetts: Addison-Wesley.

Newman, William M.
1973 *American Pluralism: A Study of Minority Groups and Social Theory.* New York: Harper and Row.

Rinder, Irwin D.
1959 "Polarities in Jewish Identification: The Personality of Ideological Extremities." In Marshall Sklare (Ed.), *The Jews: Social Patterns of an American Group.* New York: Free Press.

Rose, A.M.
1962 *A Systematic Summary of Symbolic Interaction Theory, In Human and Social Processes.* Boston: Houghton Mifflin.

Rossi, Peter H.
1961 *Motivations for Charitable Giving: A Case Study of an Eastern Metropolitan Area.* Chicago: University of Chicago Press.

Rothman, Jack
1960 "In-Group Identification and Out-Group Association: A Theoretical and Experimental Study." *Journal of Jewish Communal Service* 37:81-93.

Segalman, Ralph
1967 "Jewish Identity Scales: A Report." *Jewish Social Studies* 29:92-111.

Shore, Marlene
1987 *The Science of Social Redemption: McGill, The Chicago School, and the Origins of Social Research in Canada.* Toronto: University of Toronto Press.

Sklare, Marshall
    1959 "The Changing Profile of the American Jew."
          Unpublished paper presented to the National Con-
          ference of Jewish Communal Service.

Stark, Rodney and Charles Y. Glock
    1968 *American Piety: The Nature of Religious Commitment.*
          Berkeley: University of California Press.

Stone, Gregory
    1962 "Appearance and the Self." In Arnold M. Rose (Ed.),
          Human Behavior and Social Processes. Boston:
          Houghton Mifflin.

Thomas, W. I. and Florian Znaniecki
    1918 *The Polish Peasant in Europe and America.* Volumes
          I/IV. Boston: The Gorham Press.

Winch, Robert F.
    1962 *Identification and its Familial Determinants.* Indianapolis:
          Bobbs-Merrill.

Wirth, Louis
    1928 *The Ghetto.* Chicago: University of Chicago Press.

Zorbaugh, Harvey
    1929 *The Gold Coast and the Slum.* Chicago: University of
          Chicago Press.

RESPONSE

Rodney Sawatsky

I am going to present more of an impressionistic response rather than a considered critique. What I am going to do is talk about the issue of Mennonite identity under various rubrics, and hopefully in the process respond to at least some of the issues Driedger has raised.

One of the ways Mennonites have pursued their identity question is, of course, through history. In *Anabaptists Four Centuries Later*, this was again an important element. In fact, when re-reading that book just recently, I was rather overwhelmed by how incredibly normative it is for a sociological work. Certainly Mennonites have viewed their past as very important to their present identity. Again and again its been said that if you want to define who and what Mennonites are, they are best understood as a people with a particular history. Key to that history are certain code words, such as the one that was redefined after World War II, "Anabaptist." "Anabaptist" became such a powerful code word in the first CMP study that it became the preeminent criterion for measuring adherence to Mennonite identity.

Now what I would like to see us examine in CMP-II is the way in which history is used to identify ourselves, how Mennonites use history, and even how they perceive the word *Anabaptist* as a self-definer. The issue is not so much one of saying what it means to be Anabaptist, or that Mennonites ought to be Anabaptist, but rather to what extent this term has now become so much a part of our identity that immediately when the word is mentioned we all genuflect because there's something magical about it. This suggests an interesting dynamic that has developed in our Mennonite culture by way of identity with the code word *Anabaptist*. So I'm interested in discovering to what extent and how we look to history to define ourselves, as evidenced particularly in our use of Anabaptism.

Another area in which we do our identifying is in terms of theology, or what Driedger called ideology. In CMP-I, a variety of indices were used. I dislike the fundamentalist index profoundly. I think it is not very useful because on that index, I suspect, I and almost everybody else here is a fundamentalist. The fundamentalist index just does not discriminate. Perhaps a more valid index would look like a "Moral Majority" index or some other way by which we could get at some of those other areas of identity that would discriminate better. Rather than asking "Do you believe in the infallibility of the Bible?" we would ask "Does Israel retain a major role in God's providence?" We could tap into other streams of North American thought that are not simply from the 1940s but are very much alive in the 1980s.

Another kind of identity is, of course, that of ethnicity, which is a major focus in Leo's paper. James Juhnke has made the point in several of his papers that the preeminent variable in North American Mennonite history is the fact of the two dominant ethnic groups--Swiss/South German and Dutch/North German--and that these must be taken more seriously. His point of reference for this is the turn of the century, and I wonder whether this difference is still true in the 1980s. Do North American Mennonites see themselves primarily in terms of one or the other of these two dominant ethnic traditions? And if so, have we been focusing too much on the differences between Mennonite denominations? Is denomination really the most important variable? Or is the more interesting variable or an equally interesting variable that of the two Mennonite ethnic streams? Are Mennonites who come out of a Dutch-Prussian-Russian tradition different from Mennonites who come out of a Swiss-South German tradition? If so, to lump all of the congregations and members of the General Conference Mennonite Church together is going to run into major problems because this denomination includes both of these major ethnic groupings. It may be that people from these two ethnic groups respond quite differently. We don't know that for certain, but it is certainly worth checking.

When we talk about ethnicity, there are immediately all kinds of implications one of which Leo mentioned, namely, the greater variety of ethnicities in the Mennonite church today. I'd be interested to know, when we talk about the Quebecois situation, to what extent Quebec Mennonites identify themselves more as Quebecois than as Mennonites? How do they see themselves? Or do we worry very much that the Chinese Mennonites insist on encouraging a Chinese culture in their churches? We spend a lot of time thinking about ethnicity in relation to our Pennsylvania Dutch or Low German cultures which may be equally applicable in relation to other, newer Mennonite ethnicities.

With regard to the ethnicity question, I think we have to take seriously John Redekop's book, *A People Apart: Ethnicity and the Mennonite Brethren*. We may have quarrels with Redekop concerning his definitions and methodology, etc., but how do we define Mennonite? And how do the people in our communities perceive themselves as Mennonite or understand their various identities? Does a Mennonite have to be a member of a Mennonite church? Can one be a Mennonite and be a member of a Presbyterian Church? Or can one be a Mennonite and even be an atheist? It's going to be difficult for us to get hold of some of these variables. Because CMP-II is only going to survey the members of Mennonite churches, it cannot test for Mennonite identity outside the congregation. We should be finding ways also to survey those people who may identify themselves as Mennonite but are not in Mennonite churches.

I recently wrote the article defining "Mennonite" for the fifth volume of the *Mennonite Encyclopedia*. In trying to work at the religiosity-ethnicity issue there, I had to reflect on the fact that we tend to consider our children to be Mennonites before they are baptized if they are raised in the church but at what point do they cease being Mennonites if they decide not to be baptized? When they are 25 years of age, or 35? If we have the notion that he or she may decide to be baptized when they are 45, we might say that the nurturing process just takes a long time. Meanwhile, do we consider such persons Mennonite? And if not, why not? Are children prior to baptism not Mennonite?

In all of this I'm trying to indicate relative to John Redekop's book that our definition of Mennonite depends in part on whether we have a revivalistic notion or a more nurturing understanding of how one progresses into the Mennonite church and the role that early socialization plays in either case. And so the question that we need to work at in our research is how we and our people perceive what it means to be Mennonite.

Now for a few comments about Mennonite identity and nationality. I think that we need better indices of the differences between Canadian and American Mennonites. The reason is that we sometimes assume that Mennonites can somehow avoid the influence of national culture because they are Mennonite. Such an assumption is one of unwarranted pride to think that somehow we can avoid the socialization process of our public education, the particular national history we are taught, and the kinds of mythologies we imbibe in our schools. Our national identity needs to be taken much more seriously because we are all socialized in terms of the myths and biases of our national cultures.

Then there is identity by regions, which I cannot discuss at any
length here, except to ask: are California and British Columbia
Mennonites essentially the same by virtue of their west coast
environmental influences? Some would say "yes," arguing that they
are much more alike, regardless of denominational affiliation (MC,
GC, or MB) than are Mennonites of whatever stripe in Kansas or
Pennsylvania.

Then how about identity by various communities? There's
some of that in CMP-I, but I think this needs to be probed at greater
depth also. What are the important relevant communities to which
we relate? Is is primarily the church, or might our primary identity
be found in our professions or friends in the workplace or the labor
union, or a political organization? It will not yield enough information to ask only to what organization persons belong. We need more
of a sense as to how involved persons are and how much of their
identity comes from these other communal sources. This, of course,
is a subtle thing and more difficult to assess.

Another source of identity, if I can trust my observations from
living in a house with teenage children, is the mass culture that penetrates even our family life. For my teenagers, a most important
influence in developing identity is mass culture--rock music, football,
soap serials on television, etc. All of these and many more
influences need to be probed to know what the forces are that in fact
are shaping and determining the identity, not just of our kids, but of
adults as well. For instance, the question, have you watched a particular soap serial more than five times in the past year? may be revealing. It's not only going to be the 18 year olds who are going to say
yes, they have watched "Young and Restless" that many times, but
it's going to be housewives and perhaps many elderly people who are
sitting there doing the same thing while their kids are at school. This
is not unrelated to the impact of religious television on our people
and how this element of mass culture is influencing us and shaping
our thought patterns.

I made an earlier comment with reference to theology. Let me
add here that I think we need to look at such things as our worship
styles which are influenced by religion on television--the way that
religious services are seen as entertainment events, which has now
become a dominant mode in Mennonite churches. Church music
has to be entertainment. How important is it for persons "to be
blessed" in their worship services, and what does it mean "to be
blessed"? It may refer to how much entertainment value it had for
them. These kinds of questions are important if we want to gauge
the theological outlook of the person in the Mennonite pew. These
are more important, I suspect, than intellectual assent to orthodox

beliefs.

In conclusion, I would encourage the researchers to replicate no more than fifty percent of the former questionnaire and that a lot of new material be introduced. I don't think that in seventeen years the longitudinal analysis is going to help much anyway. We need all kinds of new questions to determine who Mennonites are today.

RESPONSE

Jose Ortiz

I am responding to this paper not as a sociologist but as a Hispanic educator. To me there are two symbols that express the corporate life of Mennonites, especially the ones that came to North America from Europe. One is the Bible, originally black leather bound in the German language; the other is the *Martyrs' Mirror*. These were household properties, two symbols of continuing great significance to me in my life.

Now when I look at the Mennonites of America, there are likewise two symbols that express their Mennonite historical and sociological identity. One is the *Mennonite Encyclopedia*, and the other is the Kauffman-Harder book, *Anabaptists Four Centuries Later*. But in this case, I had to say to Howard Kauffman when that earlier research was done that we Hispanic Mennonites were the members "missing in action," and that applies to the contents of the *Mennonite Encyclopedia* as well. But now I'm glad to hear that both works are being revised.

If Rod Sawatsky's response to Leo Driedger's paper was impressionistic, mine will be by way of the Hispanic case study. I have opted to reflect on the Hispanic experience in the Mennonite Church, although by so doing I may seem to be bypassing Leo's paper. Hispanics are just about 2.2 percent of the Mennonite Church (MC) population. We constitute about 2,400 members in 55 congregations. I've heard it said that we are the fastest growing part of the Mennonite Church, but I regret to report that this is not the case anymore. We have recently lost some congregations and we are on a church growth plateau at present.

There is one way that we are a repetition of your own ethnic diversity because we are composed of Mexicans, Puerto Ricans, Santo Dominicans, Chilians, and Cubans, just as you are composed of Swiss, Prussian and Russian Mennonites, not to mention the African and Asian Mennonites. Yes, assimilation is occurring. In my family we have assimilated through intermarriage, and I have six nephews who are Anglos. Two of my sisters married Anglo fellows, and so I have nephews with the names of Hershberger and Brenner; and if you want to "play the Mennonite game" with me, I can do that too.

Schooling has been another way of assimilating. We now have thirty graduates from our Hispanic program at Goshen College and about forty new Hispanics enrolled each year.

Our assimilation into Mennonite church life is through the conversion experience and into the folklore of your community; for when you engage in your Mennonite relief sales, food booths, and other things, we are there too. Thus we are assimilating not only by way of our hearts and brains, but by our stomachs also.

When Leo talked about the melting-pot type of assimilation, I had to ask the unspoken question, "But where is the fire coming from?" For me the fire is not coming from the Anglo Mennonites. You people are cool! We Hispanic Mennonites tend to be more fiery, especially in our worship services. But now neither is the fire coming from our Hispanic Mennonite offices. At one point we were in a rush to get offices in the Mennonite establishment, but not so much anymore. Once there, we started to pull away again, a kind of new period of disinvestment because the fire was not there. Where do we go to find the fire? The Mennonite Central Committee? Mennonite Voluntary Service? We who come from a culture of economic deprivation easily identify with MCC and VS, except that with us, considering the chronic poverty of our people, service is not just a matter of two years, it is a matter of a life time. North Americans speak about the Depression of the 1930s. We speak of the Depression of the 1930s and 1940s, 1970s and 1980s, and the coming 1990s.

So your symbols are not quite as vital for us anymore as we ask again, "Where is the fire?" Will the fire come because there is such a positive impression of Mennonites in our North American society? I was taken by a taxi driver from the airport to one of the motels, and he asked me, "Where are you going?" I said, "I am going to a Mennonite meeting." And he said, "How did you get hooked by those *hombres?*" I was at Indiana University for one of their evening courses, and I said that I was a Mennonite working here in Goshen with the Mennonite General Board. My professor, who is Jewish, said to me, "Hey, you Mennonites own all the land." Trying to think biblically, I replied, "We harvest the crops, but we don't own the land!" So there are times now when the world out there looks at us Mennonites and asks, "When are you guys going to fly out of the parental nest?"

Surely we have many things to value in the Mennonite experience, and I will mention some of them from my point of view. First, as a person who came to the Christian faith through Mennonite missions, our place of commonality is the cross of Jesus Christ. Other elements might be nonessential, but not this one.

Second, we Hispanics appreciate your orientation toward the family. To us that is also an essential part of the believers' faith. In spite of the Anabaptist notion of individual salvation, faith is a family experience. That appeals to us Hispanics because we also have a strong family tradition.

Third, we can readily assimilate into the life of your church because of your holistic approach to the Christian life. Not only the salvation of the individual but also a Christian communal emphasis on education, health, mutual aid, and other wholesome aspects appeal to us and bring us all together.

I'll conclude with some admonitions about assimilation from my point of view. You seem to have a kind of romantic approach to us Hispanics, trying to relate your ethnic experience to ours. You say, "We left Europe and came to America, learned the English language, and became North Americans, just like you." You suppose that we are going through the same process, but to this I have to reply, "Wait a minute." This is not exactly my experience. When I came to America, I was already an American citizen. I came to America not to form a New Netherland or New Brunswick or New York, or a Berne, Switzerland, in Indiana, or an Alexanderwohl, Russia, in Kansas, for there was already a San Antonio, a Santa Fe, and a San Juan Capistrano here. When you people came to America , you cut your ties with Europe; but I did not have to cut mine with Puerto Rico. I continue to go back and forth. Yes, we also assimilate, but we continue the two-way traffic as we associate with our San Antonios and Santa Fe. You people seem more ready to cut your ties with Europe than we with Latin America. We are more suspicious of assimilation, and when it happens with us, it is for a more explicit reason and perhaps only for a season. In our history, we may be more conscious that we have options. At times we find strength in assimilation, and at other times not. So we intentionally continue to be bilingual and bicultural; and once in awhile we just like to be by ourselves! That is part of our ethos, while your ethos appears to us to be more affected by the melting pot.

I would also say that when it comes to the question of assimilation, I have a second opinion because somehow you have managed in the last fifteen years to diffuse such things as leadership, which is such a strong component in Hispanic churches. In his paper Leo asked what it takes to keep people together. With us, leadership is one of the most important factors, while you seem to have diffused this factor. And so in this respect also, perhaps, we are running counter to the leveling influences of the American culture.

Let me conclude by repeating that Hispanics can affirm the necessity of assimilation; but for us it is more of a consciously negotiated assimilation, not an unconscious melting pot process.